THE
FRIENDSHIP
PACK

*Open the Gift of Friendship
and Learn the Secret of the
Native American Medicine Bag*

GREY WOLF AND ANDY BAGGOTT

JOURNEY EDITIONS
BOSTON • TOKYO • SINGAPORE

First published in the United States in 1999 by Journey Editions,
an imprint of Periplus Editions (HK) Ltd, with editorial offices at
153 Milk Street, Boston, Massachusetts 02109

Design copyright © The Ivy Press Limited 1999
Text copyright © Grey Wolf and Andy Baggott 1999

The Catalog Card Number is on file with the Library of Congress

ISBN 1-885203-80-2

Distributed by

USA	Canada	Asia
TUTTLE PUBLISHING	RAINCOAST BOOKS	BERKELEY BOOKS PTE LTD
Distribution Center	8680 Cambie Street	5 Little Road #08-01
Airport Industrial Park	Vancouver	Singapore 536983
364 Innovation Drive	British Columbia	Tel: (65) 280-3320
North Clarendon	V6P 6M9	Fax: (65) 280-6290
VT 05759-9436	Tel: (604) 323-7100	
Tel: (802) 773-8930	Fax: (604) 323-2600	
Tel: (800) 526-2778		

This book was conceived, designed, and produced by
THE IVY PRESS LIMITED

Editorial Director: Sophie Collins
Art Director: Peter Bridgewater
Managing Editor: Anne Townley
Project Editor: Rowan Davies
Editor: Mandy Greenfield
DTP Designers: Louise Howell and Ginny Zeal
Illustrators: Michaela Bloomfield, Kim Glass, Lorraine Harrison,
Valerie Kieffer, Jaqueline Mair, Sarah Young
Picture Researcher: Vanessa Fletcher

Reproduction and printing in Hong Kong by
Hong Kong Graphic and Printing Ltd.

This book is typeset in 9½pt Monotype Janson
First edition
05 04 03 02 01 00 99   10 9 8 7 6 5 4 3 2 1

CONTENTS

INTRODUCTION

The Algonquian peoples lived far and wide across North America. Their lands were diverse and varied, which makes it impossible to talk comprehensively about the whole Algonquian people, so we shall concentrate in this book on the tribes and villagers of the east coast. These were the first people to come into contact with white settlers, and it was their interaction with neighbors and newcomers that earned them their reputation as the "masters of friendship."

Among the tribes of the Algonquian, just as in the rest of the world, there was trade between people of varied cultures and languages. Cross-cultural communication can be fraught with difficulty, especially if there is no common language. Misunderstandings and miscommunications are frequent, and it is these that can lead to conflict and war.

The Algonquian largely overcame this problem by understanding and developing friendships. Friendships create connections between human beings, allowing them greater knowledge of each other and establishing boundaries of acceptability; they give individuals common ground. Such friendships among the Algonquian were cemented with gifts and exchanges; they were formed not out of "niceness," but out of necessity. The diversity of the land on which they lived meant that different tribes had different needs, many of which had to be met through trade and exchange. War was generally not an option, for it threatened the very survival of the tribe. The Algonquian understood the wealth and happiness that result from peaceful coexistence. They were just as human in their failings as we are today—the difference was that they understood the significance of friendship.

The Algonquian understood the importance of giving gifts as a means of establishing mutual trust— the basis for fair trading and peace.

The Algonquian were a diverse people who understood the true meaning of friendship.

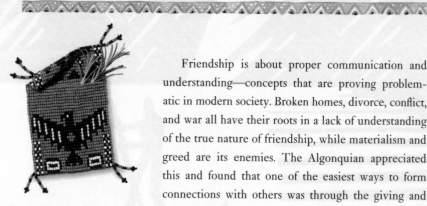

Friendship is about proper communication and understanding—concepts that are proving problematic in modern society. Broken homes, divorce, conflict, and war all have their roots in a lack of understanding of the true nature of friendship, while materialism and greed are its enemies. The Algonquian appreciated this and found that one of the easiest ways to form connections with others was through the giving and receiving of gifts.

The "friendship bag" will act as a constant reminder of the need for good communication, and the objects you keep in it will help you improve your relationships with others.

This book aims to reveal the true meaning of friendship and to show how understanding it can enrich every aspect of your life. It will show you that materialism and greed are not the way to happiness and fulfillment, and that by understanding yourself better and learning to be less attached to physical things your life can become more harmonious.

The friendship bag, or medicine bag, contained within this pack is a tool for developing and establishing friendships. You will be given clear instructions on its significance, its historical roots, and, most important, its practical use in modern society. The friendship bag creates connections between humans on many different levels and helps to open new lines of communication.

The Friendship Pack places the Algonquian in their historical and cultural context, showing how these so-called primitives have influenced much of modern-day society with their wisdom and knowledge. The Algonquian were not savages; on the contrary, without their openness and their willingness to share their knowledge with white settlers, the first arrivals in the "New World" would certainly not have survived, and the United States as we know it today would not exist. The legacy left to us by the Algonquian people is a legacy of wisdom and understanding that is timeless.

Because friendship was the foundation of all exchange, trade, and knowledge between the Algonquian, their culture is among the richest and most diverse in the world. Understanding and communication lay at the root of every aspect of their

existence, from their dealings with the Dutch, French, Swedish, and English to their own ancient myths and beliefs. A common thread of wisdom seems to be woven throughout everything.

A "friendship bag" may contain stones, shells, animal and bird artifacts, or any number of other items of significance to the owner.

This pack is not a short history book with a Native American keepsake; it is a vibrant instruction manual about how to live a happier and more harmonious life. It represents an opportunity for you to change for the better and to learn from the wisdom of an ancient people. Since it is a book about friendship, it does not explore the negative aspects of Native American history, but considers the positive lessons that can be gleaned from an extremely old culture.

If you approach this book with an honest heart, searching for the truth, you will be able to reap much from it. *The Friendship Pack* opens a door to understanding the world, in a way that is as relevant today as it has always been. We trust that you will step through that door with us, and that this book may help you to better understand the true nature of friendship. If you choose to search, you will find a more enriching way of living that is not dependent on race, gender, religion, or status, but only upon the love and compassion that lie within each of us.

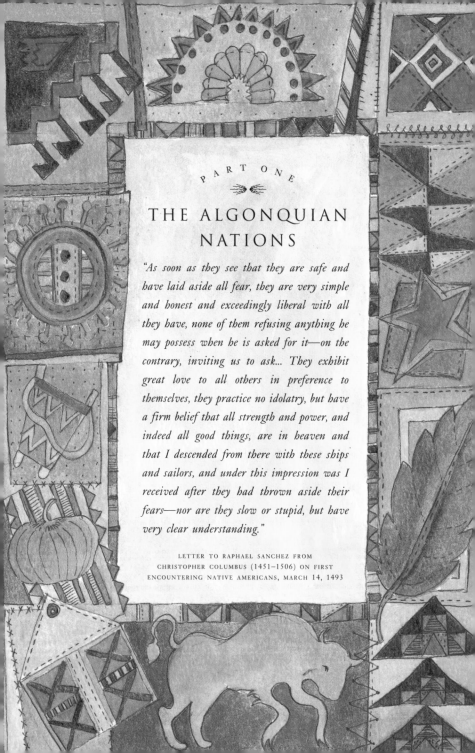

PART ONE

THE ALGONQUIAN NATIONS

"*As soon as they see that they are safe and have laid aside all fear, they are very simple and honest and exceedingly liberal with all they have, none of them refusing anything he may possess when he is asked for it—on the contrary, inviting us to ask... They exhibit great love to all others in preference to themselves, they practice no idolatry, but have a firm belief that all strength and power, and indeed all good things, are in heaven and that I descended from there with these ships and sailors, and under this impression was I received after they had thrown aside their fears—nor are they slow or stupid, but have very clear understanding.*"

LETTER TO RAPHAEL SANCHEZ FROM
CHRISTOPHER COLUMBUS (1451–1506) ON FIRST
ENCOUNTERING NATIVE AMERICANS, MARCH 14, 1493

WHO ARE THE ALGONQUIAN?

The tribes that inhabited North America when the white settlers arrived had migrated there thousands of years beforehand. The Algonquian were the first nations to have contact with white explorers and colonists, but their own origins are unclear, although it is believed that they probably migrated to the eastern coast from the north and west of the continent.

THE ORIGINS OF THE ALGONQUIAN

The term Algonquian refers to a linguistic group of Native American nations who inhabited North America. Shown on the map overleaf are the locations of eighteen of these tribes, which represent only a fraction of the original vast number of Algonquian nations. Some groups consisted of only a single small village; some comprised several villages; and others extended over a greater area.

The written history of the Algonquian begins after the arrival of the white settlers; however, the latter brought with them many new diseases which decimated some of the tribes. So by the time that white settlers began writing down the history of the Algonquian, some of the smaller groups—who had lost many members to the new diseases—had already been integrated into the larger ones. Despite this, there remained many differences among the Algonquian tribes.

This painting portrays the tranquillity of the friendly Native American hunter, who was at peace with his environment.

THE PLAINS TRIBES

The most famous of the tribes were those that inhabited the western plains, a vast area stretching from the foothills of the Rocky Mountains in the west down to the Mississippi valley in the east. These Plains Natives were hunter-gatherers who had a nomadic lifestyle and lived in tepees. They are the Natives featured in old Wild West movies. They followed the herds of buffalo that grazed on the grasslands, and among these Plains Natives were Algonquian nations (*see p.14, nos. 7–9*).

THE GREAT LAKES TRIBES

In contrast, the peoples who lived around the Great Lakes—such as the Cree, the Ojibwe, Huron, Sauk and Fox, Illinois, and Kikapoo (*see p.14, nos. 10, 12–16*)— inhabited a very different environment from that of their Plains relatives, relying for their means of survival on trapping and trading. They had no need to go hunting on the plains, because the Great Lakes and surrounding areas provided them with all that they required. They hunted elk and trapped beaver, and were expert fishermen.

Since the Great Lakes tribes had no need of a nomadic lifestyle, they lived in fixed homes constructed of timber poles covered with birch bark (*see p.19*). In those times, before deforestation, birch trees grew to enormous sizes: a single tree could be so large that it would take three men with their arms outstretched to encircle the trunk. Birch bark was also used as a covering for the canoes in which the Great Lakes tribes traveled the waterways.

Tribes who lived around the Great Lakes were expert fishermen who traveled the waterways in birch-bark covered canoes.

ALGONQUIAN HABITATS

To UNDERSTAND THE CULTURAL DIVERSITY AMONG THE TRIBES OF THE ALGONQUIAN, YOU NEED TO UNDERSTAND THE RANGE OF TERRITORIES OVER WHICH THEY WERE SPREAD. IF YOU LOOK AT THE MAP, YOU WILL SEE THAT THE ALGONQUIAN NATION COVERED A VAST, AND TOPOGRAPHICALLY DIVERSE, AREA.

KEY

 MOHAWK   CHEROKEE

IROQUOIS   ALGONQUIAN

MAIN ALGONQUIAN NATIONS

1 POWHATAN	10 CREE
2 DELAWARE	11 ALGONKIN
(LENI-LENAPE)	12 OJIBWE
3 PEQUOT	13 HURON
4 MASSACHUSET	14 SAUK & FOX
5 PENOBSCOT	15 ILLINOIS
6 MICMAC	16 KIKAPOO
7 CHEYENNE	17 WAMPANOAG
8 ARAPOHO	18 SHAWNEE
9 BLACKFOOT	

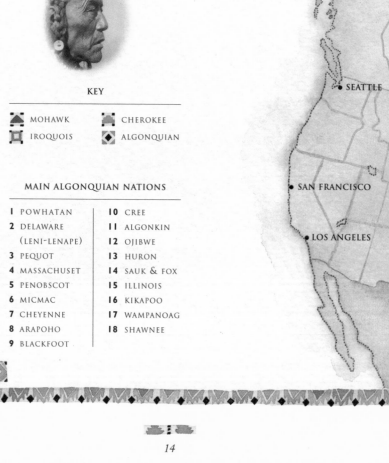

SEATTLE

SAN FRANCISCO

LOS ANGELES

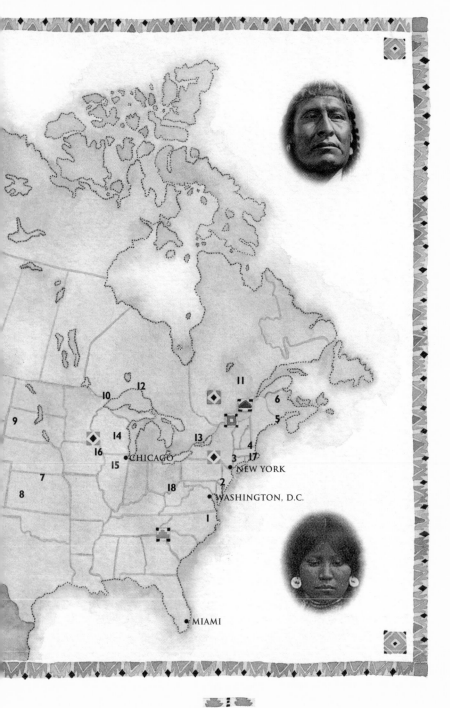

10

12

11

6

9

5

14

13

16

4

15

•CHICAGO

3

17

•NEW YORK

7

18

2

8

•WASHINGTON, D.C.

1

•MIAMI

THE IROQUOIS CONFEDERACY

On the map you will notice a large area, comprising the St. Lawrence lowlands, lying between the coastal Algonquian tribes and the Great Lakes tribes. The Iroquois Confederacy—a highly structured confederacy of five non-Algonquian peoples— filled this gap and we shall discuss it in greater detail later (*see p.34*).

THE COASTAL TRIBES

The nations located along the eastern seaboard (*see p.14, nos. 1–6, 17*) were the first to meet the incoming Europeans or, as one group called them, "the salt-water people" (because, to these Native Americans, the Europeans were not of the land but of the sea). These coastal groups lived along the banks of large rivers, such as the Delaware and the Hudson, and their ways of living were radically different from that of the more inland groups: less nomadic, more settled and agricultural.

There was thus great variation—both in geographical location and in lifestyle— between the coastal Algonquian living in the east and the Plains Natives living in the continental landmass to the west. Likewise, there was enormous diversity between the northern and southern tribes, which becomes especially apparent when looking at the differing lifestyles of the coastal tribes.

Foraging for fruit and nuts constituted a large part of indigenous life on the eastern coast of North America.

The Micmac (*no. 6*) and the Algonkin (*no. 11*) peoples lived in the far north in a distinctly temperate climate. They dwelt on a longitudinal parallel with the British Isles, but with one major difference: the weather in Britain benefits from the influence of the warming Gulf Stream, while the tribes of the northern part of America enjoyed no such benefits. Their growing season was very short, so they were semi-nomadic and had to rely more on hunting-gathering and less on farming than their southern relatives. Nevertheless, they lived in fixed villages, unlike the indigenous peoples of the High Plains, although they did have to spend long periods away from home on hunting and foraging expeditions.

Moving farther south, the tribes of the Penobscot, Massachuset, Wampanoag, Pequot, Delaware (Leni-Lenape), and Powhatan (*see p.14, nos. 1–5, 17*) were much more developed as farmers, owing to a considerably warmer climate and longer growing season. These were the nations that met and had many dealings with Dutch, Swedish, and British settlers.

The rich culture of the coastal tribes had a profound effect upon the first European colonists to encounter their "cult of friendship."

When talking about the culture of friendship in the early years of colonization (1580s–1680s), the coastal peoples were in many ways the most significant because they represented the first point of contact for the early explorers and colonists. They had been settled in the same area for thousands of years and had a rich culture, which had a profound influence upon those who associated with them. These tribes maintained an open-door policy to all who came to their lands, while the only time they left home themselves was to trade.

THE ALGONQUIAN TRADE ROUTE

Trade was the one thing that bound the Algonquian and other similarly diverse nations together. Along the mountain range that is today known as the Appalachians, which runs from northern Maine all the way south to the Gulf Coast via western Georgia, lay the major trade route known as the Appalachian Trail. This route was used by many trading nations, including the Cherokee, the Iroquois, and several Algonquian tribes. Many of the modern roads running through these mountains, including the famous Blue-Ridge Parkway of Virginia, still follow the old Algonquian trade routes.

DWELLINGS

Algonquian dwellings depended for their structure on the type of lifestyle—nomadic or settled—of the tribe in question.

The peoples of the settled or stationary Algonquian nations lived in permanent homes of pole construction, known as wigwams. These were constructed on a framework of poles or saplings—in the winter, covered with three or more layers of rushes or birch bark. A traditional Micmac wigwam, for instance, was covered with cedar-bark fiber, and overlaid with overlapping strips of birch bark and grass matting. In the summer, a lighter covering, or two layers over a conical lodge, would suffice; in the south, dwellings might be thatched with leaves of the palmetto, a fan palm indigenous to the southeastern areas.

Tepees were lighter constructions with walls made of buffalo hide, used by nomadic Algonquian peoples. They would normally be positioned with their backs toward the prevailing wind, three-pole structures generally being more sturdy than the four-pole variety.

Tribes such as the Blackfoot decorated their dwellings with elaborate patterns of birds and animals, some of which might have appeared to them in visions and dreams. Such images offered protection to those who lived under them, and reflected the medicine power of the owner.

THE NAMING OF THE DELAWARE

THE DELAWARE TRIBE WAS NAMED AFTER ONE OF THE COLONIAL LEADERS, LORD DE LA WARR (1577–1619), AN ENGLISH LORD WHO—AFTER SERVING UNDER ROBERT, 2ND EARL OF ESSEX (1566–1601)—WAS APPOINTED FIRST GOVERNOR OF VIRGINIA IN 1610. THE RIVER OF THAT REGION WAS FIRST NAMED AFTER HIM, AND CONSEQUENTLY THE PEOPLE WHO LIVED BY IT AND THE STATE THROUGH WHICH IT PASSED.

Several Algonquian tribes followed river or mountain trails to trade goods. Routes that Native Americans once used for trading purposes are now modern roads.

EXCHANGE, TRADE, AND CULTURE

The tribes living in the southern region of the eastern seaboard (*see p.14, nos. 1–5, 17*) grew cotton, tobacco, sweet potatoes, beans, corn, and squash. They enjoyed a long growing period and could often sow and reap two harvests in one season. All their crops formed items of trade, but the Native Americans also possessed various trade materials that were not readily available farther north. The soil in the south was rich in clay, and the indigenous tribespeople were accomplished potters, which skill in turn produced valuable barter.

The more northerly hunter-gatherer Natives, who did not enjoy such fertile soil, traded in furs and skins. Tribes such as the Huron (*no. 13*), the Micmac (*no. 6*), and the Algonkin (*no. 11*) were hunters and trappers who exchanged their furs for the crops that they could not readily grow in their own lands.

Tribes living in the southern region of the eastern North American coast ate very well because of the long growing season and abundance of food.

Likewise, the Great Lakes tribes (*nos. 10, 12–16*) bartered with fish and beaver skins for the coastal peoples' crops, which they could not grow; however, they did have a ready supply of wild rice to harvest. By bending its willowy grass over their canoes and lightly tapping it so that the grain fell into them, they managed to collect a very valuable trade item while leaving unharmed the plants that would produce the next crop.

In this way, external exchanges built up by which the Powhatan traded extensively with the Cherokee, the Delaware with the Iroquois, and so on. Communication with the non-Algonquian tribes was not a problem: many of the Algonquian were multilingual. Among the Algonquian themselves, the basic language was the same—only the dialect and accent varied from tribe to tribe.

THE CULTURAL TRADITIONS

There were common roots among the Algonquian: for example, the Leni-Lenape, the Powhatan, and the Shawnee were all once part of one nation. They originally lived in the Lenape homeland, and archeologists and anthropologists have now, to some degree, verified their migration patterns to the eastern woodlands of North America. When the Europeans arrived, the Leni-Lenape were located in the area that today forms Delaware, Pennsylvania, and part of New York State.

They did not possess a single, unifying government, but rather small divisions in which a chief or holy-man was in charge of one or more villages. Marriage and trade between villages were common and this created links between the different peoples. In addition to standard trade items such as pots, crops, skins, and furs, many other items were traded, including baskets made from willow or reed, and flint tools. The Leni-Lenape and the Powhatan were both matriarchal societies (*see pp.28–9*). The men were primarily hunters, while the women were farmers. Their farms could extend up to 200 acres/80 hectares and their maintenance required extremely intensive labor.

Some Algonquian tribes, such as the Leni-Lenape, were matriarchal societies. Native American communities often followed the lead of the female in matters beyond childbearing.

THE FIRST CONTACTS WITH EUROPEANS

In 1524, Giovanni da Verrazano (1485–1528), an Italian navigator working for France and searching for a northwest passage to Asia, entered New York harbor through the strait that now bears his name (the Verrazano Narrows). He anchored off Staten Island and it is recorded that he met the native people there.

In 1602, Bartholomew Gosnold (d. 1607) met Algonquians in the vicinity of Martha's Vineyard and Elizabeth Island (*see p.38*). The next recorded contact, with the Leni-Lenape, came in 1609, when Captain Henry Hudson (c. 1550–1611), sailing for the Dutch, landed in New York harbor (*see p.36*).

It was these early explorers who provided the first historical records of contact between white men and the indigenous peoples of North America.

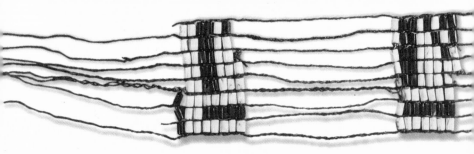

THE WAMPUM BELT

I F YOU HAVE SEEN THE FILM "THE LAST OF THE MOHICANS," YOU MAY REMEMBER THE SCENE IN WHICH DANIEL DAY-LEWIS WALKS INTO THE VILLAGE OF THE HURON PEOPLE. IN THAT SCENE, HE CARRIES A BEAD BELT AND DECLARES THAT IT CONTAINS THE HISTORY OF HIS ANCESTORS—THE STORY OF HIS FATHER, HIS FATHER'S FATHER, AND SO ON. IT WAS A WAMPUM BELT.

THE WAMPUM BELT WAS A UNIVERSAL MEANS OF COMMUNICATION BETWEEN THE MOHICAN, THE ALGONQUIAN, AND THE IROQUOIS. ALL THESE NATIVE PEOPLES COULD COMMUNICATE BY MEANS OF WAMPUM BELTS. THE SYMBOLISM OF THE TUBULAR BEADWORK SPOKE A LANGUAGE THAT EVERYONE UNDERSTOOD. THE PATTERNS WERE AS READABLE TO THE NATIVE AMERICANS AS THE SCRIPT OF THIS BOOK IS TO US. AT THAT TIME, THE INDIGENOUS PEOPLE WERE NOT SKILLED IN THE USE OF PAPER AND INK, BUT THIS DID NOT MEAN THEIR HISTORY WENT UNRECORDED. INDEED, THE CONSTITUTION OF THE IROQUOIS CONFEDERACY WAS WRITTEN ON WAMPUM BELTS.

North American Natives helped early European colonists to survive bitter winters on the eastern seaboard.

The beadwork on a wampum belt was a code for Native Americans. It could be read like the words of this book.

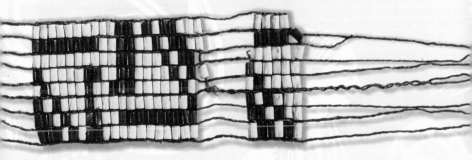

THE BUILDING OF FRIENDSHIPS

To understand the nature of friendship, one needs to understand the Native American concept of the world. They regarded every natural item—food, fur, wood, shells—as a gift from the Creator and from Mother Earth. This meant that they did not consider trade to be the swapping of essentials, but rather the exchange of gifts.

They believed that the only reason the Creator gave them these gifts in such abundance was so that they could be shared, and the more they shared, the richer they would become. Someone who had a great deal to share—and who shared it unselfishly with others—was highly respected by the Algonquian people. This was integral to the web of life of which we are all a part.

The home and all of their possessions were seen by Native Americans as being gifts from the Creator and from Mother Earth, which were meant to be shared unselfishly with other people.

THE PEACE PIPE

The Algonquian, like all the other nations of the eastern woodlands, and particularly the Iroquois, centered around what was known as "the long house" or "the big house" in their villages. In this large structure, which became the focal point of the community, the people met to converse and take part in their ceremonies, one of the most important of which was the tradition of the sacred pipe.

The pipe was a feature of all the different tribes who inhabited that region and, because it facilitated a point of contact, it became known as "the peace pipe." Each nation, and indeed each individual, had—and to this day still has—its own particular way of using the pipe, which might have become a source of conflict, but the indigenous peoples of North America realized that friendship is formed from common bonds, not from differences. As a result, when Native Americans of differing traditions met, they would share and celebrate what was common to them, rather than focus on their disparate customs.

> " WHEN THIS PIPE TOUCHES YOUR LIP, MAY IT OPERATE A BLESSING UPON ALL MY TRIBE. MAY THE SMOKE RISE LIKE A CLOUD AND CARRY AWAY WITH IT ALL THE ANIMOSITIES THAT HAVE ARISEN BETWEEN US. "
>
> *Black Thunder, a native of the Fox tribe, at a treaty meeting in 1860*

The tradition shared by all the various tribes and nations was one of peace, of making connections, and the pipe played an integral part in its rituals. Clay pipes made by the southern tribes have been found in areas as far north as those inhabited by the Ojibwe, the Huron, the Algonkin, and the Micmac, where no clay was available, which indicates that the pipes must have been traded. From that trade arose the ceremony of sharing the pipe and the tradition of making peace, which became so ingrained among the Algonquian.

Sharing a pipe became a sacred activity and symbol of peace because the many different tribes of the Algonquian nation used it to facilitate contact with others.

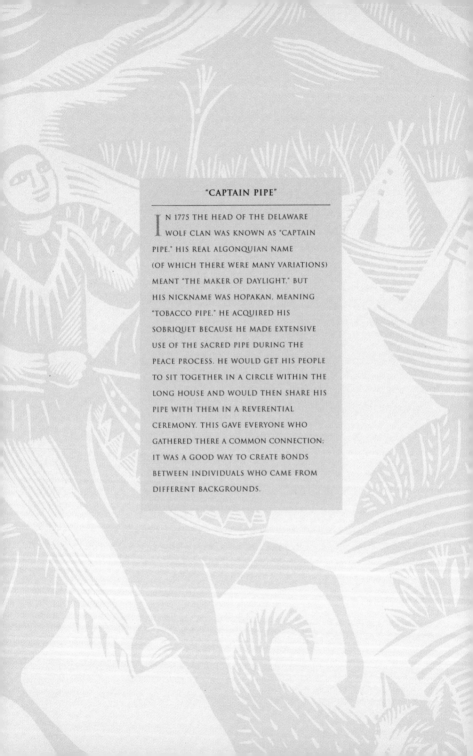

"CAPTAIN PIPE"

IN 1775 THE HEAD OF THE DELAWARE WOLF CLAN WAS KNOWN AS "CAPTAIN PIPE." HIS REAL ALGONQUIAN NAME (OF WHICH THERE WERE MANY VARIATIONS) MEANT "THE MAKER OF DAYLIGHT." BUT HIS NICKNAME WAS HOPAKAN, MEANING "TOBACCO PIPE." HE ACQUIRED HIS SOBRIQUET BECAUSE HE MADE EXTENSIVE USE OF THE SACRED PIPE DURING THE PEACE PROCESS. HE WOULD GET HIS PEOPLE TO SIT TOGETHER IN A CIRCLE WITHIN THE LONG HOUSE AND WOULD THEN SHARE HIS PIPE WITH THEM IN A REVERENTIAL CEREMONY. THIS GAVE EVERYONE WHO GATHERED THERE A COMMON CONNECTION; IT WAS A GOOD WAY TO CREATE BONDS BETWEEN INDIVIDUALS WHO CAME FROM DIFFERENT BACKGROUNDS.

THE GIVE-AWAY

The give-away was a ceremony in which the pipe would be passed and gifts exchanged. It was a matter of honor that anyone who entered an Algonquian village—be it to trade, to seek a wife, or for any other reason—would be given gifts and would always carry with them presents to exchange. Often when someone arrived at a village, they would be carrying in one hand a wampum belt, to prove who they were and to show their lineage, and in the other hand a gift for the *sachem* or village elder.

This gift might be something that was of relatively little value to the giver, since it would be an item commonly available in his or her own village, but of great value and rarity to the receiver. To a southern Native, pottery was commonplace, while good-quality, thick beaver pelts were rare; to a lakeside Native, on the other hand, the opposite was true. So when a southern Native arrived in a lakeside village, his gift might be a pot or a clay pipe and he might receive in return a thick, warm beaver pelt. Both parties would then possess items of value to themselves. They would both be richer in material and spiritual terms, because they would not only have gained something for daily use but would also have cemented a friendship.

During the give-away ceremony, gifts such as this carved wooden bowl would be exchanged by the Native Americans as tokens of friendship.

This is how different indigenous peoples, often speaking different languages and having widely varying traditions, made and maintained peace. It also explains in part why the white settlers were so readily accepted by the Algonquian, because it was not their differences that were important, but their common bond as human beings. Furthermore, the settlers had unique items to exchange, which established common ground for them with the Native Americans—and it was upon this greed-free foundation that peace was built. It was only when white settlers' aims became wholly selfish that peace between them turned to conflict.

A MATRIARCHAL SOCIETY

Algonquian societies have generally been matriarchal—that is, headed by women who are held in great respect within the tribe. The tendency of most matriarchal societies is to resolve conflict in a manner far less invasive to the well-being of their members than that of patriarchal, or male-dominated, societies. As such, the Algonquian had a vastly different outlook on the "manly" pursuit of war.

A woman held in high esteem within a tribe often found ways to resolve conflicts that ensured everyone's well-being and avoided battles.

There were some intriguing ways in which Native North American nations resolved disagreements and settled disputes, which seldom involved either the shedding of blood or death. One such means was the game of lacrosse. Some accounts of the history of the game credit its origin to the Iroquois, but it was in fact played by a large spectrum of indigenous peoples, including the Algonquian.

In times past, lacrosse acted as a version of warfare—and even the Native North Americans, who traditionally favored negotiation over conflict, had occasional disputes over subjects such as land rights. If two groups of people had a dispute that could not be resolved, then a time and place were selected for battle to take place. The participants for both sides were chosen (both men and women could be involved) and at the prescribed time, the game/war would begin.

The audience would gather on the sidelines and watch the event to its end, sometimes from the rising to the setting of the sun. The side that accumulated the highest score would be the victor in this game/war and the dispute would be settled accordingly. The resolution of conflict by means of lacrosse was by no means a soft option. Many participants were injured, scarred, and sometimes even disabled, but seldom did a death occur. In fact, a death would usually stop the game, with the side that caused it automatically pronounced the loser.

This represents a typical way in which to resolve conflict in any society that has as part of its culture respect for what is feminine. The Algonquian people, as well as other nations of the Americas, listened to their women, respected their counsel, and looked upon them as equals—to the extent that many "medicine men" and chiefs were women. It was only the patriarchal attitude of the Europeans, and their refusal to deal with female Native leaders, that pushed the North American indigenous women into the background of recorded history.

Algonquian tribes often played lacrosse as a means of settling disputes, instead of resorting to open warfare.

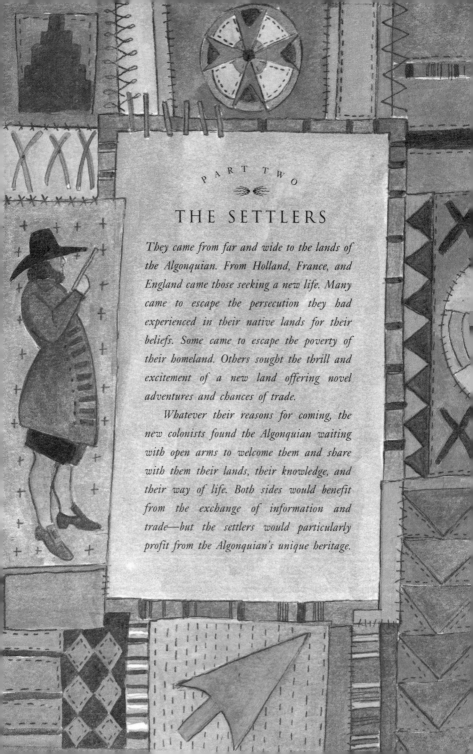

THE SETTLERS

They came from far and wide to the lands of
the Algonquian. From Holland, France, and
England came those seeking a new life. Many
came to escape the persecution they had
experienced in their native lands for their
beliefs. Some came to escape the poverty of
their homeland. Others sought the thrill and
excitement of a new land offering novel
adventures and chances of trade.

  Whatever their reasons for coming, the
new colonists found the Algonquian waiting
with open arms to welcome them and share
with them their lands, their knowledge, and
their way of life. Both sides would benefit
from the exchange of information and
trade—but the settlers would particularly
profit from the Algonquian's unique heritage.

OPEN-ARM POLICIES

Trade brought new ideas and skills to Native American villages. When the first thick, warm beaver pelts arrived at the coastal villages from the Great Lakes tribes, long before the arrival of the white settlers, the coastal Natives needed to learn new skills, because they had no experience of working with pelts. Likewise, when the first clay pipes arrived in the northern coastal villages from the south, this catalyzed a period of learning, as the tribes assimilated new ways to honor and commune with the tobacco plant, which was sacred in their culture and was used as a prayer-carrier (*see p.82*).

Native Americans were always eager to discover new things, and, if a stranger arrived with unfamiliar items, he or she would be embraced with open arms and great rejoicing, for the novelties signified a time of advancement and learning for the tribe. The coming of the white settlers was seen as nothing less than an opportunity to make new connections, establish new trades, and learn new skills.

The arrival of the white settlers was viewed by the Natives as a chance to barter goods and acquire new trade items.

No part of an animal was left unutilized by the indigenous peoples, as this Blackfoot scalping knife with its bear's paw hilt proves.

Perhaps the most versatile of Native American weapons, the pipe tomahawk could be used for smoking or cutting firewood as well as killing.

Many years before the white explorers arrived in America, the Iroquois people had undergone thirteen generations of bloody conflict. Their area was inhabited by five main tribes: the Mohawk, the Seneka, the Oneida, the Onondaga, and the Cayuga, and the whole region was surrounded by members of the Algonquian nation. These five tribes were constantly in conflict, competing for hunting lands and fishing rights, and razing each other's villages to the ground.

In the mid-sixteenth century, there was a member of the Iroquois named Dekanawidah, who was one of the first Native Americans of his nation to turn his thoughts toward peace. He had a vision of a "tree of the great peace" (*see p.50*). This vision showed him that all of the feuding tribes should stand under the tree and, provided they remained beneath it, there would be no further conflict. It was his idea to form the Iroquois Confederacy, which was to become the first constitutional democracy in the modern world.

Dekanawidah was not gifted with the capacity for strong and powerful speech. Nor did he have the ability to speak with authority, and, in a land of little writing and much talking, a poor orator is ignored. He tried to explain his vision, but his words fell on deaf ears. However, one day he met a Huron Native named Hiawatha, who spoke the Algonquian language, but was also well-versed in the language of the Iroquois. He listened as Dekanawidah explained his formula for peace.

Having heard Dekanawidah's words, and recognizing their potential power and wisdom, Hiawatha agreed to speak to the Iroquois and, being an accomplished orator, to explain Dekanawidah's vision. He traveled to all of the villages of the Iroquois nation and spoke for peace, and the people listened. For the first time in hundreds of years, peace came to the people of the Iroquois and, thanks to Hiawatha's efforts, the Iroquois Confederacy was formed.

THE COMING OF THE FRENCH

The French were not the first white settlers to arrive in America (the English preceded them by about twenty or thirty years, *see p.38*), but their contribution to the lives of the Native Americans, and their later significance in North American history, deserve mentioning here. When the French arrived in America in the early 1600s, they brought with them items that changed the lives of the indigenous peoples. The most significant of these items were metals: the French introduced steel for tipping arrows, brass for making tomahawks, and tools that made life so much simpler for the Native Americans.

After coming to the American east coast, the first French explorers traveled along the St. Lawrence and Ottawa rivers to the lands of the Algonkin. The Ottawa River formed the center of the waterway system and river trade routes for the area. Tribes would leave from here to spend the winter roaming the lands and waterways in small bands, hunting and gathering, and would then return in summer to meet in large groups in order to share experiences and to trade. When the French arrived with new and wonderful items, they were readily accepted by the Natives as just another trading group. The fact that they had a different skin color, and a different language and culture, was not impor-

French pioneer and explorer Samuel de Champlain (1567–1635) is known as the founder of Quebec, Canada, established in 1608.

> **"** WE, WHO ARE CLAY BLENDED BY THE MASTER POTTER, COME FROM THE KILN OF CREATION IN MANY HUES. HOW CAN PEOPLE SAY ONE SKIN IS COLORED, WHEN EACH HAS ITS OWN COLORATION? WHAT SHOULD IT MATTER THAT ONE BOWL IS DARK AND THE OTHER PALE, IF EACH IS OF GOOD DESIGN AND SERVES ITS PURPOSE WELL? **"**
>
> *Polingay, a Native of the Hopi tribe*

tant. What was important to the Algonquian were the elements that both peoples had in common, and in particular the items that the French had to trade. Thereafter, the French traveled on to the lands of the Huron and the Ojibwe and cemented new trade links among the Great Lakes tribes.

DEALINGS WITH THE DUTCH

In 1609, the English navigator Henry Hudson, sailing on behalf of the Dutch East India Company, was trying to find a northeast passage past Russia. When his crew rebelled upon entering the ice, he was forced to double back, turning west toward America, and in early September 1609 sailed into what has become New York harbor. Here he sent men ashore, who encountered some

Peter Stuyvesant (1592–1672) was director of the New Netherlands colony in North America, which later became New York State.

of the indigenous people and invited them back to their ship to trade. One officer wrote in his account that the Natives were "very polite, yet we dared not trust them"—wise words, for a few days later those same Native Americans, believed to have been Iroquois, attacked several members of the ship.

A few days later, the Algonquian living on Manhattan Island met the sailors. On September 12, Hudson himself went ashore to meet them, recording in his journal that they were "very good people, for when they saw that I would not remain, they supposed that I was afraid of their bows and, taking their arrows, they broke them into pieces and threw them into the fire."

Hudson then sailed his ship, the *Half Moon*, all the way up the Hudson River to modern-day Albany, establishing Dutch claims to the area later to become the center of the Dutch colony known as "New Netherland." Near Albany, in 1624, the Dutch Fur Trading Company established its first trading post in America, calling it "Fort Orange."

The following year, the Dutch West India Company established a colony on Manhattan Island, naming it "New Amsterdam." In its first year there, it was able to send 4,000 beaver pelts and 700 otter skins back to The Netherlands, giving it a high profit margin. And in 1626 Peter Minuit (1580–1638), the governor of New Amsterdam, purchased Manhattan Island for sixty gilders' worth of goods.

When the Dutch switched their trading allegiances to the Iroquois, who could provide even more pelts, as well as other trade items, they fell into conflict with the local Algonquian tribes. Not only that, but the Dutch joined the Iroquois in raids on the Algonquian villages, betraying the friendship that had been so freely offered to them.

THE FAILURE OF THE DUTCH COLONIAL EFFORT

The Dutch colonial effort was short-lived for two reasons: mismanagement and profiteering. Greed and friendship do not mix. By 1664, no longer having the support of the Native Americans, the Dutch had lost the Connecticut Valley to the English and only barely managed to keep the Delaware Valley from the Swedish, who wanted to colonize it too. In September 1664 James, Duke of York (1633–1701), who was later to become James II of England, forced the Dutch governor, Peter Stuyvesant, to surrender New Amsterdam to the English, after which it was renamed New York in recognition of its change of ownership. This marked the end of Dutch control of these lands, and the arrival of the Quakers in America.

New Amsterdam on Manhattan Island was lost by the Dutch to the English after they betrayed their Algonquian friends. It later became New York City.

DEALINGS WITH THE ENGLISH

In 1584, Sir Walter Raleigh (or Ralegh, as he spelled his own name) was issued a royal patent by Queen Elizabeth I (1533–1603) to "discover, search, find out, and view such remote, heathen, and barbarous lands, countries, and territories not actually in possession of any Christian prince." Raleigh (1552–1618) sent an exploration party to Virginia, headed by Arthur Barlowe and Philip Amadus. It landed at Roanoke Island, from where Amadus wrote after an encounter with the Native Americans, "We were entertained with all kindness and found the people most gentle, loving, and faithful, free of guile and treason, and living in the manner of the Golden Age."

Elizabeth I, Queen of England, made Sir Walter Raleigh her agent for finding "heathen" territories that were not claimed by other Christian countries.

In 1584, Sir Walter Raleigh sent the first explorers to Virginia, named after England's so-called virgin queen.

In 1585, the first English settlers were sent over, but the colony failed within a year. Two years later, John White (fl. 1585–93) established another settlement at Roanoke—it too was to fail, because of lack of supplies from England. The first English explorers had congenial dealings with the Native Americans, especially around Cape Cod, so named by Bartholomew Gosnold in 1602 for its abundance of fish.

Two of the Native Americans who met these early explorers and learned English from them were Samoset (d. 1653, a member of the Pemaquitt tribe) and Squanto (d. 1622), who later toured England.

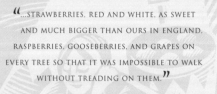

"...STRAWBERRIES, RED AND WHITE, AS SWEET AND MUCH BIGGER THAN OURS IN ENGLAND, RASPBERRIES, GOOSEBERRIES, AND GRAPES ON EVERY TREE SO THAT IT WAS IMPOSSIBLE TO WALK WITHOUT TREADING ON THEM."

Bartholomew Gosnold, describing Martha's Vineyard in 1602

THE POCAHONTAS STORY

In 1606, under the "London Virginia Company," a colony was successfully founded in Jamestown, Virginia. John Smith (1580–1631), a young but seasoned explorer, was sent there in December 1606 as military commander and one of the council of governors. His fellow-governors considered Smith too young and inexperienced for the job and had him in irons by the time they arrived in the "New World" in 1607. But Jamestown was located in a mosquito-infested swamp that was ill-suited to colonists trying to establish a foothold in a strange land, and their leaders soon found themselves forced to seek the help of the imprisoned explorer.

Smith was duly released and went to meet the chief of the Powhatan to seek aid from the Native peoples. Although Chief Powhatan was himself in favor of helping the colonists, other members of the tribal council were less inclined to assist them and imprisoned Smith, sentencing him to death. As he was about to be executed, Pocahontas, the twelve-year-old daughter of Chief Powhatan, stepped forward and intervened to stop the execution, physically throwing herself onto Smith to protect him, knowing that no one would dare to strike the daughter of a chief. Her brave action averted the execution and led to the Powhatan granting aid to the people of Jamestown.

THE TOBACCO TRADE

Between 1607 and 1609, over 900 colonists were sent to the Jamestown colony in Virginia, but by 1610 there were fewer than 100 colonists—described by Smith as among "the laziest of men" he had ever seen—still alive. They were saved by the arrival of Lord de la Warr (*see p.19*), who accompanied 150 new colonists to take up the post of governor. The new settlers were more inclined to hard work and, with the assistance of the Powhatan, were able to farm the land and provide food for themselves.

By 1612 the colony was doing well and its success was further enhanced when John Rolfe (1585–1622), one of the new colonists, discovered how to turn tobacco into a cash crop. Now the colony had something to trade, a means of purchasing essential tools and supplies, and a way of expanding. Thus the Virginia tobacco industry was born.

Native stockades of this kind were copied by early English colonialists to protect their stores from attack and to confine their animals.

THE PILGRIMS

In October 1620, a group of separatists arrived in Massachusetts from England on the *Mayflower*. They had left their homes in Yorkshire and Lancashire to escape religious persecution, and became known as "the Pilgrims." The first tribe they met was the Wampanoag, who welcomed the visitors, taking them into their own homes and feeding them, thus enabling them to survive the winter in this new land. In March 1621, Samoset (*see p.38*), chief of the Pemaquitt, walked into the colony, greeting them with "Welcome, Englishmen." He then sent for Massasrit, the Wampanoag chief, and for Squanto (*see p.38*). A treaty was made with Massasrit, who felt that peace was preferable to war in dealing with strangers, allowing the Pilgrims to stay on his land—a treaty that lasted for forty years.

In the fall of 1621, after the first harvests, the Native Americans and the Pilgrims found that they shared a long-established tradition: the harvest festival. The Pilgrims invited the local tribes to join their celebration, as a token of thanks for all of their help. And so the American holiday known as "Thanksgiving" was born.

THE QUAKERS

In 1681, William Penn (1644–1718), a Quaker reformer and preacher, was given the right by King Charles II (1630–85) to establish a colony in the Delaware area, which became known as "Pennsylvania." It proved to be a peaceful, prosperous colony, for Penn had gone to great lengths to establish good relations with the Native tribes. He signed a treaty with the Leni-Lenape, allowing each colonist to claim an area of land whose size was dictated by the distance he could walk into the woods in a single day. The colony was further increased in 1736 because of the efforts of Conrad Weiser (1696–1760), a second-generation colonist who eventually extended the settlement into the Susquehanna Valley in the land of the Iroquois.

The *Mayflower* brought the Pilgrims to New England, where the Wampanoag tribe shared their land with them.

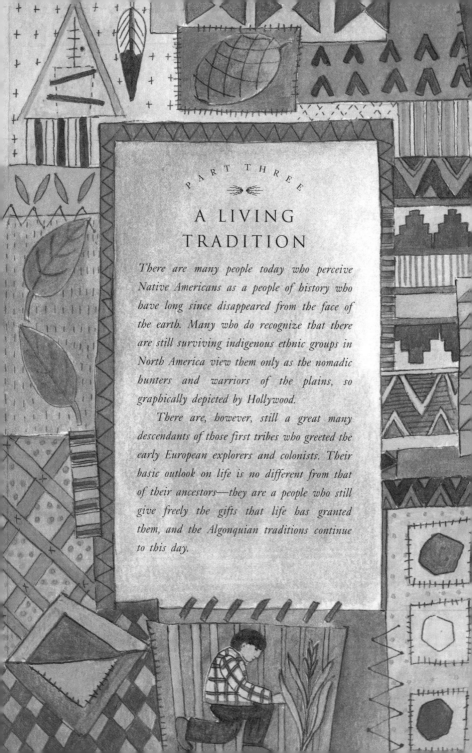

PART THREE

A LIVING TRADITION

There are many people today who perceive Native Americans as a people of history who have long since disappeared from the face of the earth. Many who do recognize that there are still surviving indigenous ethnic groups in North America view them only as the nomadic hunters and warriors of the plains, so graphically depicted by Hollywood.

There are, however, still a great many descendants of those first tribes who greeted the early European explorers and colonists. Their basic outlook on life is no different from that of their ancestors—they are a people who still give freely the gifts that life has granted them, and the Algonquian traditions continue to this day.

WHERE ARE THEY NOW?

The Algonquian still exist (and some of them were, indeed, those Native Americans depicted by Hollywood), although the vast numbers of Algonquian tribes have been greatly reduced. When the first colonists arrived in America, they brought with them not only more effective weapons (the rifle, for instance, had been invented by August Kotter in 1520)—which in turn made the casualties of war much higher—but a variety of diseases to which the Native Americans had no natural resistance. They also brought with them on board their ships disease-carrying vermin such as rats and cockroaches, which had never been found in North America and had a very detrimental effect on the indigenous tribes.

There are still Natives in America of wholly Algonquian descent, like the elder above, who was the last surviving member of his tribe.

Many Native Americans died from minor illnesses like colds and influenza, because they had no natural immunity to such ailments. Lung diseases and smallpox decimated the Algonquian population, and in some cases wiped out whole villages. For example, it is estimated that the Micmac, who had little experience of illness and fevers until the arrival of the white settlers, decreased in population from about 4,000 to approximately half that number by the early eighteenth century because of smallpox and other diseases.

The many conflicts, from the early wars between Natives and colonists (such as the French and Indian War of 1754–9), through the American Civil War of 1861–5, two World Wars, Korea, Vietnam, and the Gulf War, also had a devastating effect on the indigenous populations throughout North America, and the Algonquian were not exempt from this.

Today the east-coast Algonquian nations are largely no more, although there are some reservations with Algonquian still living on them. There are also a number of people who can claim ancestry from Algonquian nations that are no longer officially recognized by the U.S. government. There are Algonquian reservations in Massachusetts, New Hampshire, Vermont, and Maine, but there are probably more

Algonquian living outside reservations than on them. They live in mainstream American communities in all fifty states and may not even be recognized as being Algonquian by their communities. They are doctors, lawyers, teachers, and construction workers. You could find Algonquian anywhere and never be aware of their ancestry unless they decided to tell you about it. The largest population of east-coast Algonquian people to be found in one area today is the Delaware (or, more correctly, the Leni-Lenape), who live in Oklahoma (*see overleaf*).

Native Americans have been relocated from their original territories many times by the descendants of the European colonists who took their land.

THE DELAWARE

The Leni-Lenape, later known as the Delaware (*see p.19*), were known by the other Algonquian peoples in the area as "The Grandfathers" and were considered the oldest of the Algonquian tribes. It was the Leni-Lenape who called the new colonists *swannuken,* or "salt-water people." In 1600, they were living in the Delaware River Valley from Cape Henlepen northward to the west side of the lower Hudson Valley—a vast area that ran from New Jersey and most of Pennsylvania into New York State. The Leni-Lenape were not nomadic and, according to archeologists, appear to have lived in this area for several thousand years.

During the following 300 years, they were relocated by the colonial and later the federal authorities at least twenty times. By 1900, they had already been relocated, at various times, to Arkansas, Delaware, Indiana, Kansas, Louisiana, Michigan, Missouri, New Jersey, New York, Ohio, Oklahoma, Ontario, Pennsylvania, Texas, West Virginia, and Wisconsin. After 1900, they were regarded as having been absorbed into the Cherokee nation and to be living primarily in Oklahoma, and in 1979 the federal Bureau of Indian Affairs "administratively terminated" the Delaware Nation.

It was not until September 1996 that the Bureau gave the Delaware "official" recognition, allowing them once more to separate themselves as the Delaware tribe of Native Americans, and ended their classification as Cherokee. They now have their tribal offices in Bartlesville, Oklahoma. There are currently 2,000 Munsi, another division of the Leni-Lenape, living on three reservations in southern Ontario, Canada. There are a further 1,500 descendants living as members of the Munsi-Stockbridge tribe in northern Wisconsin and a mixed Munsi-Ojibwe community living near Ottawa, Kansas.

The federally recognized Delaware tribes in Oklahoma accept only two eastern groups as also being Delaware: the Sandhill-Lenape and the Nanticoke-Lenape. However, the Ramapough Mountain Native Americans who live in New Jersey, and number about 2,500, may also be of Lenape origin. There are also a large number of mixed-bloods among the tribes, making federal recognition difficult to acquire.

■■ **The oldest Algonquian tribe, the Delaware, has recently forced the federal authorities to return its name to it.**

THE ABSENTEE DELAWARE

ANOTHER GROUP THAT IS FEDERALLY
RECOGNIZED IS THE DELAWARE TRIBE
OF WESTERN OKLAHOMA, OR THE
"ABSENTEE DELAWARE" AS THEY ARE
SOMETIMES KNOWN. THEY NUMBER ONLY
ABOUT 1,000 AND REPRESENT THE
REMNANTS OF A GROUP OF DELAWARE
WHO WERE RELOCATED TO TEXAS. THEY
NOW HAVE THEIR TRIBAL HEADQUARTERS
IN ANADARKO, OKLAHOMA.

CONNECTIONS TO NATURE

The Algonquian felt a deep respect for, and link with, all of creation. They regarded everything as being both part of the web of life and unique. A stone, a plant, or an animal was acknowledged as being part of a larger creation and yet was honored for its individuality. The same was true of humans. Each human being was seen as unique, and yet, at the same time, as just another strand of the web of life.

Native Americans respected nature, and North America once had many dense forests like this one, with trees much larger than they are today.

This meant that differences in the appearance, customs, and traditions of various peoples were accepted without prejudice by the Algonquian, because the web of the world was seen as being made up of millions of interconnected parts, all of which could be readily accommodated.

THE "STANDING PEOPLE"

The Algonquian view of trees, or the "standing people" as they called them, was very different from modern Western perceptions. Each tree was acknowledged as being part of creation and, therefore, sacred. This did not mean that it was not to be used, but that it was not seen merely as a resource to be chopped down without care or thought. A tree was regarded as having a spirit or energy, which deserved to be honored. Offerings such as tobacco (*see p.82*) were used in ceremonies before a tree was felled.

Trees provided materials for houses, canoes, weapons, tools, food—in the form of fruits and nuts—and many utensils. Birch bark (*see pp.19, 54–5*) and maple syrup were resources that could be harvested without damage to the tree, if done correctly. And wherever possible the Algonquian would manage their woodlands responsibly, so there would be plenty of wood for future generations.

When the white colonists arrived in America, respect for trees waned. The settlers viewed trees as an unlimited source of raw materials for the home and for ship-building, giving little thought to future generations. One of the most significant reasons why Britain was able to expand her domain so successfully was due to the trees that her colonists were able to harvest from the Algonquian lands, for the creation of an enormous merchant navy.

A tree was seen by Natives as a being, to which one should give something back for all of the gifts it gave from itself.

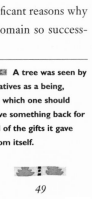

THE TREE OF THE GREAT PEACE

"I am Dekanawidah and, with the Five Nations confederate, I plant the Tree of the Great Peace.

I name the tree: the Tree of the Great Long Leaves. Under the shade of this Tree of the Great Peace, we spread the white, soft feather-down of the globe thistle as seats for you, Atotaroh, and your cousin lords.

Roots have spread out from the tree, and the name of these roots is the Great White Roots of Peace. If any man of any nation shall show a desire to obey the laws of the Great Peace, they shall trace the roots to their source, and they shall be welcomed to take shelter beneath the Tree of the Great Long Leaves.

The smoke of the confederate council fire shall pierce the sky so that all nations may discover the central council fire of the Great Peace.

I, Dekanawidah, and the confederate lords now uproot the tallest pine tree and into the cavity thereby made, we cast all weapons of war. Into the depths of the earth, down into the deep under-earth currents of water flowing into unknown regions, we cast all weapons of war. We bury them from sight forever and plant again the tree."

Translation of a story told by the Iroquois
about the beginning of the Iroquois Confederacy (see p.34)

(see p.34)

Before the British arrived in America, most of their ship masts were made from Norwegian spruce, with the size of the mast being dictated by the size and height of the trees. Many of the masts had to be spliced from two trees, and there was a maximum size that could be created in this way, which limited the overall size of the ships they were able to build. In America, the colonists found many trees to be much taller than those they had previously been able to acquire. They could now make masts that were much bigger from a single tree, which in turn meant that much larger ships could be built. This led to the British being able to transport much expanded cargoes of people, supplies, and commercial goods. But the home-building exploits of the colonists and the harvesting of trees for England's shipyards laid many areas of the eastern woodland completely bare.

THE PLANT PEOPLE

Plants other than trees were also regarded by Native Americans as having a spirit, and the three main crops of corn, beans, and squash were known as "the three sisters." Plants were intrinsic to the survival of the Algonquian, and these three sisters would also become major food sources for the modern world, along with the other main crop grown by the indigenous peoples: the potato.

Plants also provided medicine, and often the medicine man or woman of the village would "journey" in a shamanistic trance to meet the spirit of a plant and learn from it how best to utilize its healing energies. This idea of learning by communicating with the spirit of a plant is a resource that has been lost to modern Western civilization, although there has recently been a surge of interest in herbal remedies. In this modern age of ecological disasters, deforestation, and global warming, we could learn a great deal from the Algonquian people and from their respectful attitude toward the natural world that lies around them.

▨ Shamanist trances probably led the Natives to name their staples corn, beans and squash "the three sisters."

ANIMAL ALLIES

To the Algonquian, the animal kingdom was much more than a mere source of food and furs. It was a vibrant part of creation that had unlimited lessons to teach humans. The Algonquian would observe animals and then commune with the spirits of those whose characteristics they desired in their own lives. For instance, if a warrior was seeking strength, he might hope to learn this from the spirit of the bear. If he was seeking clear vision, he might contact the spirit of the eagle. The otter, a sociable animal, could teach lessons of sharing and the value of being nonjudgmental, whereas the buffalo was regarded as being symbolic of abundance.

Dreams and visions were seen as significant tools of communication. If an animal appeared in a dream to an Algonquian, he would seek to learn what that particular animal was trying to teach him. This he would do through a combination of

Animals like the stag, eagle, coyote, and bear were so much a part of the lives of Native Americans that they felt a kinship with them.

observation of its characteristics and communing with its spirit. Spiritual journeying to meet spirit beings was part of normal practice for the Algonquian; it played an important role in enabling them to view life from more than one perspective.

> WE LOVE QUIET, WE SUFFER THE MOUSE TO PLAY. WHEN THE WOODS ARE RUSTLED BY THE WIND, WE FEAR NOT.
>
> *Unknown Native (probably a Delaware) to the governor of Pennsylvania in 1796*

THE STONE PEOPLE

FLINT WAS USED EXTENSIVELY BY THE ALGONQUIAN FOR ARROWHEADS, AXHEADS, AND OTHER TOOLS. THE ALGONQUIAN WERE HIGHLY SKILLED IN THEIR FASHIONING OF FLINT AND WOULD OFTEN SEEK THE GUIDANCE OF THE SPIRIT OF A STONE CONCERNING HOW IT COULD BEST BE PUT TO USE. OTHER STONES AND CRYSTALS WERE ALSO USED IN MEDICINE: THE ALGONQUIAN WERE WELL AWARE OF THE HEALING PROPERTIES OF CRYSTALS, WHICH OFTEN CONSTITUTED IMPORTANT HEALING TOOLS IN THE MEDICINE BAGS OF ALGONQUIAN HEALERS (SEE PP. 80-1).

Flint was shattered into fragments, then shaped by the indigenous people into tools.

Much birch-bark art was practical as well as decorative; this Ojibwe scroll is either telling a story or depicting a journey.

BIRCH-BARK ART

A specialty of the woodlanders' art—and one closely associated with their desire for harmony with nature—was working with birch bark. The bark was extremely soft and pliable, which meant that it could easily be rolled, bent, engraved, or stitched, and the pink inner layer could be scraped away to create all manner of patterns and shapes. It was made into a variety of containers and boxes, particularly by the Micmac, who excelled at decorating such boxes with an enormous range of designs—circles, squared circles, diamonds, scrolls, points, concentric motifs, and outlines—and used natural dyes and sophisticated quillwork to complete them.

Bark rolls inscribed with pictographs were also a major component of the Ojibwes' Grand Medicine Society, or *midewiwin,* ceremonies and were used to record the instructions, songs, and teachings of the society. They were handed on from generation to generation, with the elders instructing candidates in the intricate meanings of the pictographs. While the bark rolls were meaningless to the uninitiated, those with the necessary knowledge could read them like books. Some bark rolls were as extensive as 2½ x 1 ft./75 x 30 cm; they were inscribed with a bone stylus, and their pictures illustrated the evolving nature of the *midewiwin* ceremony. As Nhenehbush, a supernatural trickster taking on human form, is supposed to have remarked, "Ojibwe lore marked the birch as his tree, figuring the bark with its characteristic graceful pattern that reminds the Thunderers to observe respect." Since the bark of the birch tree is not only water-proof but also fire-resistant, it would not easily be set on fire if the tree was struck by lightning by the Thunderers, or guardians of fire.

Birch-bark prints were another interesting variation, which unfolded to display a repeated pattern, created by Native women piercing the bark or biting patterns into it, then letting the light pick out the designs as the bark swung in the air. Birch-bark art was widespread among many of the woodland Algonquian tribes, for practical as well as decorative purposes, while the barks of other trees—such as the cedar and slippery elm—also had consid-erable value, being used as buckets, dishes, bags, and mats. Later on, birch bark was even cut to form templates for bead designs in the shape of simple leaves, flowers, animals, birds, and figures.

PORCUPINE QUILLWORK

Another decorative device, thought to have been invented by an eastern Algonquian, was porcupine quillwork, which was taken to its most sophisti-cated, controlled form by the Cree people. Before the introduction of beads, they used quillwork to embellish garments, adding bands of it across the chest, shoulders, and cuffs. After being prepared, the quills could be sewn, braided, chained, or spliced to create work that was smoother in texture than basket

This exquisite 4in/10cm box was made from long porcupine quills, birch bark, and native dyes by the Micmac tribe.

braiding. They could then either be applied directly to an item or, for larger garments such as tunics and leggings, could be made as a separate band and then attached to the garment. The quills were dyed with natural pigments, until the introduction of commercial dyes brought with it a greater color spectrum.

MYTHS AND BELIEFS

The ancient stories of any civilization or culture are reflections of its beliefs and principles. Anecdotal stories and legends are made up of lessons that people want their children—and outside contacts—to learn so that all who associate with them will know the truths that are considered of great importance to them. However, the stories of the Algonquian peoples are not didactic; on the contrary, listeners are invited to reach their own truth through their personal interpretation of the story. One listener may reach a different conclusion from another who hears the same story, but each will take away something of value.

In indigenous communities, the mother's role in passing on customs and tribal beliefs to her children cannot be underestimated.

Communal gatherings where stories were told and songs were sung ensured that historical information and spiritual instruction passed to successive generations.

BE CAREFUL WHAT YOU WISH FOR!

A group of Algonquian held a contest to decide who should have the right to visit the land of the Great Spirit and be granted a wish. It was a contest full of courage, with four men emerging victorious. Now these four men journeyed to the land of the Great Spirit and found it to be a land full of magic and delights, fairer than the mind could possibly conceive. When they arrived, the Creator said to them, "Why have you come here?"

The first one replied that his heart was evil and that anger had made him its slave; he wished to receive a gift that would enable him to be meek and pious. The second one, being a poor man, said that he was seeking wealth and riches, so that he could better share with the people of his village. The third man, who was held in very low esteem among his people, said that he was seeking a gift that would allow him to be respected by them. The fourth was a man of great vanity. He was forever preening himself and wore only the most fashionable clothes of the time. His wish was that he might become taller than any man in his tribe, and that he might live for a very long time.

Having heard the words of these men, the Creator drew out four small boxes from his medicine bag and gave one to each of the men. He told them that in each box was a gift, but that they should not open it until they reached their homes. On doing so, the men opened their boxes and found within a gift of divine perfume. The first one, the angry man, opened his box and rubbed his body all over with this scent; it made him both meek and patient. The second, the poor man, did likewise; he began to accumulate great wealth and riches. The third man found that the perfume gave him a great power that was needed within his village, so he became highly respected.

The fourth man did not get to his home. In his urgency and impatience, he opened his box before he got there and rubbed the perfume on himself. He received precisely the gift he had asked for, although not in the way he had expected. He was transformed into a pine tree—the very first pine tree—and grew to be the tallest tree in the forest and lived for a very long time.

GLOOSKAP AND MALSUM

There are many stories and myths about Glooskap and indeed, in the story of the first pine tree (*see p.58*), many Algonquian have Glooskap named as the Great Spirit whom the four Native Americans visited. Many of the legends are parables that act as warnings against arrogance, pride, foolishness, and all manner of other human failings. Glooskap is known by different names by different peoples: in some versions, he is the Great Hare, the personification of light, the god of water, wind, and snow; and he appears in various tribes' legends under the names of Manabusch, Manabozho, Messou, and Nanibozho.

For many of the Algonquian tribes, Glooskap and Malsum were regarded as the two principal gods. Glooskap was the first man, hero, trickster, and god. His brother Malsum, the wolf, was regarded as Glooskap's *alter ego*. Legend says that their mother died at birth and that from half of her body Glooskap created everything that might be considered "good"—the sun, the moon, mammals, birds, fish, and humans; from the other half of her body, Malsum created the mountains, valleys, serpents, and all manner of things that challenge people and stand in their way.

The Algonquian's two principal gods were Glooskap, depicted setting his dogs on troublemakers, and his *alter ego*, Malsum, a wolf.

Once Glooskap had finished creating, he chose a black and a white wolf to be his attendants, but so prolific and harmful did they become that he then had to wage war on the evil creatures.

GLOOSKAP AND THE BABY

Glooskap was feeling very pleased with himself, for many had come to challenge him and all had failed. The Kewawkqu, a race of giant magicians, had fought with Glooskap and lost, as had the Medecolin, who were a band of cunning sorcerers. Goblins, fiends, demons, and witches had all come to challenge him—and all had failed. As Glooskap sat swelling with pride, a certain woman came past and he could not help but boast about how there was nothing left in the world for him to subdue. The woman just laughed.

"What are you laughing at?" Glooskap inquired angrily.

"I know of one," replied the woman, "who remains unconquered and even you cannot overcome him."

"Tell me his name," demanded Glooskap.

"He is called Wasis," said the woman and added, "but I would strongly advise you to go nowhere near him."

Glooskap, knowing himself to be all-powerful, chose to ignore this warning and sought and found Wasis. Now Wasis was only a baby and, when Glooskap found him, he was sitting on the floor sucking a piece of maple sugar and singing a song to himself. Glooskap had never married, so he was ignorant of the ways of children, but this did not deter him. Full of confidence, he smiled at the baby and asked it to come over to him. The baby smiled back, but did not move. So Glooskap began imitating the beautiful song of a bird; Wasis paid him no heed and just carried on sucking his maple sugar.

Glooskap now grew very angry and, in his most terrible and threatening voice, demanded that the baby come to him immediately, whereupon Wasis burst into the most dreadful howling. Glooskap then drew upon all of his magical resources, singing songs so terrible that they had the power to raise the dead. Wasis was singularly unmoved and merely smiled at Glooskap.

Eventually Glooskap stormed off in defeat, whereupon Wasis merely cried, "Goo, goo." Now the Native Americans say that when a baby cries "Goo," it is remembering the time when it conquered the mighty Glooskap.

CLOUD-CARRIER AND THE STAR-FOLK

There was once a handsome youth named Cloud-Carrier who lived with his parents on the banks of Lake Huron. He was a smart, strong boy, and his parents felt sure that he would become a great warrior. When he reached the threshold of manhood, it was time for him to go and search for the objects that would fill his medicine bag and thus empower him, so he set off alone into the forest. By the end of the day he had journeyed far and was becoming tired, so he lay down. Just as he was about to fall asleep, a gentle voice whispered in his ear, "Cloud-Carrier, I have come to fetch you. Follow me."

He sat up with a start: there before him was a beautiful young woman.

"Follow me," she said again, with an enticing softness that made the young man yearn to be close to her. To his surprise, no sooner had he thought of being close to her than he found himself floating with her toward the heavens. Higher and higher they rose, above the trees and through the clouds, until they came to an opening in the sky that led them into a wondrous new land.

Cloud-Carrier now realized that this beautiful maiden was a supernatural being and that she had brought him to the land of the Star-People. She directed him to enter a lodge, within which he found a most impressive array of beautiful and rare weapons. Cloud-Carrier was admiring and studying these weapons when the maiden rushed into the lodge crying, "My brother is coming! Quick, hide!" and she sat him down in a corner and covered him with a scarf.

"Nemissa, my beloved sister," said the warrior as he entered the lodge, "have you not been forbidden to speak to the Earth-People? Do not think you have hidden the young man from me." Then, turning to look directly at where Cloud-Carrier was hiding, he said in a gentle and friendly voice, "Come, let us talk, young man, for if you stay hidden there, you will grow hungry."

The young man emerged, and Nemissa's brother gave him a pipe and a bow and arrows. He also gave him his sister as a wife, and they lived together for many long and happy years. In fact, their life continues to this day, as is seen in the sky when Cloud-Carrier moves the clouds around.

PART FOUR

≫⋵⋵≪

FRIENDSHIP

Various aspects of Algonquian society now form part of everyday life in many areas of the world. For instance, there are few diets, especially among First World nations, that do not include "the three sisters" of the Algonquian fields: corns, beans, and squash. And there are no democratic countries that do not, at the very least, espouse their philosophy of openness.

This part of the book is an explanation of the gift included in The Friendship Pack. *The bag is not untypical of an eastern woodland-style bag—an item that would be given to anyone who had reached the point in his or her life when such an object could be put to good use. Take this gift into your life and let it help you to grow spiritually.*

THE FRIENDSHIP BAG

As we have seen from the stories of the Algonquian, friendships are formed through the connections made between people, and the Algonquian found that one of the easiest ways to encourage this to happen was through giving and receiving gifts. Such gifts were not mere trinkets, but items of practical use. Today we form friendships in the same manner—we trade things. More often than not these "things" are thoughts and ideas rather than physical objects, but the principle is the same.

Herbs, crystals, and other natural items will make the best medicine for your friendship bag.

A balanced friendship between two people is based upon the resources and personal qualities they have to share and their ability to trade them.

QUALITY AND RESOURCES

We are each born with a reserve of resources or talents and, as we go through life, we look to improve the quality of these talents and to acquire new ones. This is done largely through the forming of friendships and relationships.

Sometimes, when you meet a stranger, you feel an instant attraction. As you talk to that person, you feel as though you have known each other for years rather than minutes, and the more you talk, the more you discover what there is to talk about and to share. What you are both doing in this situation is trading resources. If you had nothing to trade, there would be no mutual attraction. A connection is formed between you whereby you both notice that you have things to learn from one another. This is the very foundation of friendship.

If you seek to understand another person's qualities, you will find that your own life is enriched in the process. You will become a wiser and more balanced individual through the breadth of your experience and friendships.

"MUTUAL LEARNING"

When you develop a friendship, a mutual learning process takes place. In every interaction between two human beings, there is an equal and opposite number of lessons to be learned by both parties. Often, especially if you are teaching someone about something, you may forget that you have just as much to learn in return.

Any strangely shaped stone might be called "medicine." Native Americans would wrap it in buffalo hair and keep it in a "medicine bag."

Some people even believe that the reason they are in a particular relationship is because they have such a lot to teach. This is surely a mistake: they also have much to learn, but are not willing to face that fact. Instead, they try to divert attention away from the possibility of mutual learning by concentrating on teaching.

> " THE PERSON WHO MAKES NO MISTAKES IN THEIR LIVES ENDS UP AN OLD FOOL. THE PERSON WHO MAKES MANY MISTAKES, BUT LEARNS FROM EACH AND EVERY ONE, BECOMES THE WISEST OF THE WISE. FAILURE IS NOT FALLING DOWN: IT IS NOT GETTING BACK UP AGAIN. "

THE MEDICINE PATH

Life is a journey of learning. Some Native Americans call it the "medicine path," and believe that anything that comes to teach us is "medicine." Native Americans also believe that everything is significant—that everything we encounter has the potential to teach us something, if only we are willing to learn it. Therefore, everything we encounter in our lives is medicine.

Even a feather is sacred and can teach. Everything we encounter in life is educational, once we begin to walk on the "medicine path."

In the story of Cloud-Carrier (*see p.62*), we heard of a young man going on a journey to seek medicine. This was common practice among all Algonquian. As an individual journeyed through life, he or she would constantly be seeking medicine. A special stone, a colored bead, or a small gift from a friend would all be looked upon as potential medicine. The items found to be pertinent would then be carried in a medicine bag.

If an Algonquian felt a strong attraction to a particular type of animal as a teacher, he or she might carry a piece of that animal, such as a claw, tooth, feather, or piece of fur, in the medicine bag. The artifact would act as a reminder of the lessons they had to learn from the animal and would help them to recall their bonds with the natural world and the universal web of life.

The Algonquian perceived medicine as a means of making contact with the whole of creation, and if they had "strong medicine," it meant that their connection with creation was close—as it should be if they were to find peace, health, and happiness in their daily lives.

THE PURPOSE OF THE BAG

The friendship bag that comes with this book may be used as a medicine bag. As such, it represents a bag of lessons for you to carry with you, to help you learn more and so become wiser. What you actually put into the bag is entirely up to you, but it should always be an item of personal significance that has taught—or continues to teach—you something. As you learn your lessons and become wiser, you can then start to pass your medicine on to others whom you meet, to help them on their paths. Remember, though, that if you give somebody a piece of your medicine, you have the opportunity to receive an equal and opposite amount of medicine from that person in return.

As we go through life we can gain wisdom from the lessons we learn, then pass that medicine on to someone else.

For instance, if you find a stone that attracts you, this means that it has something to teach you. Pick it up and keep it in your friendship/medicine bag. All the time that you carry it with you, it will be teaching you, whether you are aware of it or not.

Later, you may meet someone and want to form a bond with him or her. As we have already seen, the best way to do this is through exchanging gifts. With this in mind, you may feel it right to give that person your stone. The moment you do this, the connection is made between you, and the trading has begun.

> " THOSE WHO HURT YOU THE MOST ARE IN FACT YOUR SOUL-MATES. "

Your gift from the other person may not necessarily come in physical form; it might come in the form of a lesson. You should not expect to receive something material in return, but rather try to learn all you can from that person. However the other person reacts to your gift—be it positively or negatively—that is part of your learning process and part of his or her gift of medicine to you.

REAL FRIENDSHIP

Real friendship is a bond between two people that is not dependent upon anything. Friends support and help each other. Friends also teach each other.

Learning a lesson is not always a pleasant experience, especially if you are resistant to learning; so friendship may sometimes mean being hurt, but through great hurt can come great learning. It is only those to whom you are close who have the opportunity to hurt you deeply and, therefore, the chance to teach you profound truths. But it is usually we who hurt ourselves.

For instance, if you are feeling happy and positive and a friend says to you, "I don't think that color you are wearing suits you," the chances are that you will not feel hurt. You will recognize that there is no malice in their statement, that they are merely expressing an opinion, and you may well reply, "I respect your opinion, but I disagree, because this is my favorite color"—and that will be that.

Sharing a peace pipe was an important part of agreements between early colonists and Native Americans.

If, on the other hand, you are tired and unhappy with your life and your friend says the same thing, you may well feel extremely upset, believing he or she has been spiteful to you and taking the comments personally. Who has changed in this situation: you or your friend?

If someone is unpleasant to you, ask yourself, "What can I learn from this?" In this way, you may be able to turn a negative attitude into a positive learning experience. Problems between friends occur only as a result of miscommunication. One or both friends might misinterpret a word or a sentence, which leads to conflict. Often an innocuous statement is taken the wrong way, or a word is misunderstood. Good communication is as fundamental to firm friendship as miscommunication is to conflict.

MEDICINE BAGS

Medicine bags have traditionally been available in a wide variety of types, sizes, and styles, and in an extensive range of designs and materials, according to the tribes to which they belonged. The southeastern Algonquian people grew cotton and wove it into fabric long before the European settlers came to the Americas, and the medicine bag included in this pack is similar to those that were made by them. The pattern is reminiscent of Algonquian designs too, although the beads that are used on it only became available to the Native tribes of North America through trade with European colonists and merchants.

On the whole, the designs and imagery of any people reflect the world that is in close proximity to them, as they view it. The great majority of painted, appliqué and beaded designs for which the woodland Natives of North America are noted reflected the fact that the natural world they inhabited was full of plants

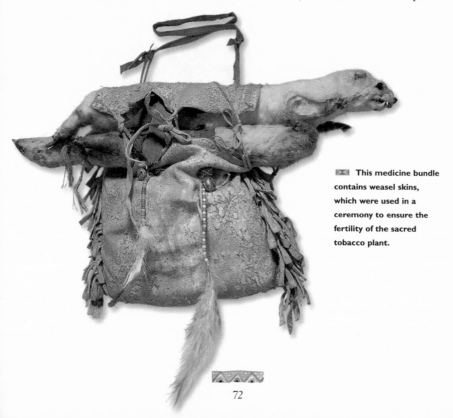

This medicine bundle contains weasel skins, which were used in a ceremony to ensure the fertility of the sacred tobacco plant.

and dense forest. As a result, their soft, curving patterns often took the shape of vines, leaves, and flowers.

The colors that the Algonquian used when painting or dyeing something also reflected those of the world around them, because the only dyes available to them were those that could be extracted from the plants and soil in their area. Their natural preference was for subtle fall colors such as brown, russet, and cream. When the Europeans arrived with their brightly coloured beads from Venice, the Native patterns and designs began to take on a new vitality.

Some larger types of medicine bags were actually known as "medicine bundles" because of their size. In these might be placed any number of items and tools that individuals would use to help them practice their medicine—items such as a "smudge fan," which was used to waft cleansing smoke from a burning herb like sage around an area, in order to prepare it for a ceremony. A medicine bundle might also hold a sacred pipe for use during prayer. Any item or tool that could be used to strengthen one's relationship with the rest of creation was considered worthy of placing in a medicine bag.

In the shaman's and medicine man or woman's bag might also be found herbal remedies used in physical healing—red willow bark, for instance, which could be chewed to relieve a headache; mint or wintergreen to settle an upset stomach; and so on.

■■■ Medicine bags come in a variety of sizes and forms. This one is made from the skin of an otter decorated with cloth, beads, and bells.

GIFTS AND CONNECTIONS

The friendship bag is a traditional artifact in which to keep items of "medicine." But what exactly is medicine and how do we learn from it?

There are many forms of medicine that it may be appropriate to keep in your bag. Crystals and animal and bird artifacts are particularly powerful medicines and can facilitate great change in an individual. One way in which this medicine works is that when you are close to an animal, bird, or stone, its vibration helps to align your own energy. For instance, if you are seeking strength, you may keep a bear claw or a stone shaped like a bear in your medicine bag, for this powerful animal symbolizes strength. If you seek to exemplify the spirit of the eagle, with its free flight and clear vision, you might put an eagle feather or talon into your medicine bag.

Plants and trees can also act as medicine. If you strive to be flexible in the way that you live—just as the willow tree is flexible in a strong wind, for instance—then you might put a piece of willow in your medicine bag. Once you have learned the quality that you desire, you may want to pass that medicine on to someone else whom you perceive to be in need of that power.

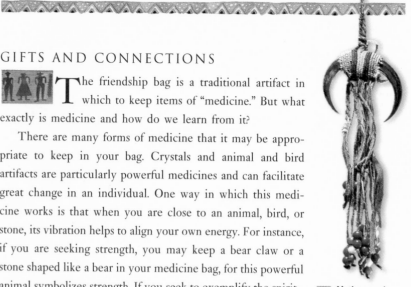

Native warriors wore tokens like this eagle talon as "medicine" in order to tap its resources.

You should never kill an animal or a bird for an artifact. You should get it from one that has died naturally. Because this will be impossible for many people, a totem or image of the creature in question—carved in wood or stone, painted on a piece of leather, or, better still, personally made by you—will work just as well.

This hide shield, showing a bear coming out of a hole and its tracks, is meant to give its owner the strength and protection that a bear conveys.

The Native American saw everything in his or her surroundings as a gift from the Creator and Mother Earth, and sought to respond in kind.

THE STORY OF SACRED OTTER

Sacred Otter was a member of the Blackfoot, an Algonquian tribe who were buffalo hunters. Just before the winter moons, Sacred Otter was out hunting with his son. Many buffalo had fallen to him, and he and his son were busy skinning their kills—so busy, in fact, that they failed to notice dark, black clouds gathering over the northern horizon.

Before they knew what was happening, the clouds flew upon them like flocks of black eagles and they were caught in the midst of the fiercest blizzard that Sacred Otter had ever known. Sacred Otter and his son tried to shelter beneath the carcass of a dead buffalo, but the chill wind blew thick torrents of snow at them and Sacred Otter knew that if he did not build a proper shelter, they would perish. So he made a small tepee out of a buffalo hide and both crawled inside. Soon the wind blew great drifts around them and the inmates of the lodge sank into a comfortable sleep.

As he slept, Sacred Otter dreamed that the snow had stopped and that he found himself outside bathed in warm sunlight. In the distance, he spied a great tepee. It was the color of golden sunlight, with a cluster of stars painted on the side, symbolic of the north. On the back was a red circle representing the sun, to which was affixed the tail of the Sacred Buffalo. The bottom of the tepee was painted the color of ice, and on its side were drawn four yellow legs with green claws, symbolic of the Thunderbird. A bright red buffalo was painted above the door, and bunches of crow feathers with small bells attached swung gently in the breeze.

Sacred Otter stood admiring this fine tepee; then a voice called out to him, "Come in, come in." Sacred Otter entered and before him stood a white-haired man, dressed all in white and with his face painted yellow, with a red line from his mouth and another across his eyes to his ears. He wore a mink skin across his chest, and around his waist were small strips of otter skin to which bells were attached. He sat before an altar on which was laid a sprig of juniper, symbolic of the sun, and silently smoked a black stone pipe.

After some time he addressed Sacred Otter as follows, "I am Es-tonea-pesta, the Lord of Cold Weather, and this yellow-painted lodge is the Snow Tepee. I control the Northlands, the winds and the snow. I saw you and your son and took pity upon you. I have medicine for you to take back to your people. Take this Snow Tepee with its symbols and medicines, this mink-skin tobacco pouch and black stone pipe. Whenever you smoke this pipe, my powers will be with you."

Then the Lord of Cold Weather showed Sacred Otter how to build the tepee and draw the sacred symbols. He also taught him sacred songs and a ceremony to make the symbols powerful. Just then, Sacred Otter awoke. Seeing that the storm had abated, he returned home with his son.

That winter, during the long cold nights, Sacred Otter built a model of the tepee he had seen in his dream; and in the spring collected the herbs he needed as medicines for the ceremony. Soon the time came for new lodges to be built, so Sacred Otter created his Snow Tepee.

The next winter, when some of the tribe were far away hunting buffalo, they were caught in a blizzard. They appealed to Sacred Otter to call upon the Lord of Cold Weather and to use his medicine. Sacred Otter took out his black stone pipe and filled it with tobacco from his mink-skin pouch. He blew smoke in the direction whence the storm came, praying, "Lord of Cold Weather, have pity on us." As he sang a sacred song, the winds abated and the snow ceased. The tribe made haste homeward, though, for they knew that the medicine would not last. As they got home, the first snow began to fall, but they were safe.

■ In a vision, Sacred Otter saw a beautiful tepee decorated with symbols that, along with holy songs and a stone pipe, would protect his tribe.

ANIMAL AND BIRD ASSOCIATIONS

It is easy to equate animal and bird behavior with our own aspirations—these creatures have strong and readily recognizable characteristics, by which we still frequently identify them in our everyday language: "strong as an ox" and "slow as a snail" being two common examples.

Here are some of the particular qualities that are associated with the animals and birds that were traditionally encountered by the Algonquian tribes. Each one may teach us something about ourselves. You may wish to obtain an image or totem of a specific animal or bird, or even create one yourself to keep in your friendship bag.

BADGER

A RELATIVE OF THE BEAR,
THE BADGER WAS TRADITIONALLY LINKED
TO TENACITY AND DETERMINATION.

OTTER

REGARDED AS THE KEEPER OF FEMININE
WISDOM, THE OTTER WAS ALSO SYMBOLIC OF
RESOURCEFULNESS.

EAGLE

THE POWERFUL EAGLE, KING OF THE BIRDS,
REPRESENTED CLEAR VISION, OBJECTIVITY,
AND A FREE SPIRIT.

DEER

THE GRACEFUL DEER TRADITIONALLY
STOOD FOR KINDNESS, KEEN SIGHT, AND
GENTLE STRENGTH.

RAVEN

THE RAVEN WAS SEEN AS A
SYMBOL OF MYSTERY. IT WAS TRADITIONALLY
ASSOCIATED WITH PSYCHIC ABILITIES.

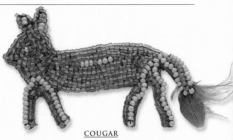

COUGAR

THE COUGAR WAS SYMBOLIC OF
LEADERSHIP AND COURAGE, AS WELL
AS ASSERTIVENESS.

MOUSE

THE MOUSE REPRESENTED
CURIOSITY, COMBINED WITH THE ABILITY
TO SCRUTINIZE ISSUES CLOSELY.

BEAVER

EVER BUSY, THE INDUSTRIOUS
BEAVER REPRESENTED BOTH
FLEXIBILITY AND CREATIVITY.

ARMADILLO

THE ARMADILLO, WITH ITS COAT OF
ARMOR, EMBODIED PROTECTION AND
PERSONAL STRENGTH.

BEAR

A SOLITARY CREATURE, THE BEAR
SYMBOLIZED POWER, WISDOM,
AND INTROSPECTION.

CRYSTAL QUALITIES

Crystals resonate with particular qualities and healing properties: some bring wisdom and understanding; some are symbolic of purity; some are cleansing; others represent creativity. People in modern industrial nations need to rediscover the special qualities that Native Americans discerned in the natural environment. Many of these crystals emit an energy that may be used by the person who holds them. But, like all medicine, you should not try to hold on to them indefinitely or their power will fade.

Below are some of the healing crystals that might have been found in an Algonquian's medicine bag, and a description of their principal qualities.

AMETHYST

THIS BEAUTIFUL PURPLE CRYSTAL WAS HIGHLY PRIZED AS A POWERFUL HEALING STONE CAPABLE OF INSPIRING SPRITUAL AWARENESS AND OF BRINGING PROTECTION TO ITS OWNER.

CITRINE

A BLEND OF YELLOW AND ORANGE, SYMBOLIZING THE COLORS OF THE EAST AND SOUTH. CITRINE WAS REPUTED TO GIVE ITS OWNERS THE WILL POWER TO ACHIEVE THEIR GOALS.

QUARTZ

SAID TO ATTRACT THE POSITIVE AND TO DISPEL THE NEGATIVE, THIS CRYSTAL WAS USED AS A HEALER, PROTECTOR, ENERGIZER, AND ALSO AS A RENEWER OF SPIRIT.

OBSIDIAN

TOOLS AND WEAPONS MADE OF THIS SHINY BLACK STONE WERE SAID TO POSSESS MAGICAL PROPERTIES AND THEREFORE TO BE ABLE TO PROTECT THEIR OWNER FROM HARM.

ROSE QUARTZ

THE LOVE STONE. ROSE QUARTZ WAS USED TO TREAT ALL AILMENTS RELATING TO THE HEART—WHETHER THESE WERE PHYSICAL, EMOTIONAL, OR SPIRITUAL AILMENTS.

IRON PYRITES

ALSO KNOWN AS "FOOL'S GOLD." IRON PYRITES WAS HIGHLY PRIZED BY MEDICINE MEN AND WOMEN, BECAUSE, FOR THEM, IRON REPRESENTED THE SOLID FLESH OF MOTHER EARTH.

FLINT

VALUED BY THE NATIVE AMERICANS FOR ITS PROTECTIVE QUALITIES, FLINT WAS USED NOT ONLY TO MAKE TOOLS AND WEAPONS BUT ALSO TO FASHION AMULETS.

AGATE

THIS CRYSTAL WAS HIGHLY FAVORED AS A PERSONAL MEDICINE STONE. IT WAS SAID TO HAVE A CALMING EFFECT AND TO AID COMMUNICATION WITH THE PLANT KINGDOM.

TURQUOISE

SACRED TO THE SKY SPIRITS, THIS CRYSTAL WAS KNOWN AS A "MASTER HEALER" AND WAS UTILIZED IN MANY ASPECTS OF MEDICINE AND TRADITIONAL NATIVE CEREMONY.

AQUAMARINE

A FEMININE STONE, AQUAMARINE WAS ASSOCIATED WITH THE ABILITY TO PRODUCE INSPIRED THOUGHTS AND WAS SAID TO CREATE A SENSE OF PEACE AND LIGHTNESS.

A PRAYER-CARRIER

Whenever you put something into your medicine bag, it should be done with honor and respect. Whenever you take something from nature, you should always leave a gift in return. This is true of all situations, whether you are taking a single berry or a whole tree, one feather or an entire bird.

One of the items that an Algonquian might carry in a medicine bag was tobacco—which was a sacred plant in their culture—in order to offer it up with a prayer in exchange for anything he or she took from nature. Tobacco was regarded as having a close link to Mother Earth and was therefore viewed as a prayer-carrier to the Creator. The Algonquian would say their prayers in a low voice, while holding some tobacco in their hand, which they would then offer to the four cardinal directions, as well as to the sky and the earth. They would promise to take no more from nature than was absolutely essential for their purpose.

The "prayer-carrier" tobacco would be smoked in pipes, like this one carved to represent a turkey buzzard, in order to send prayers to the Creator.

Such simple actions can have a profound effect upon the way that you interact with nature, setting forth your intention that you are willing to learn from Mother Earth or from any other aspect of creation that presents itself to you—you are open to the lessons it has to teach. This in turn enables you to receive great insights and wisdom. The Algonquian were a simple people whose lives were uncluttered. Ceremonies and offerings were performed in uncomplicated ways, using intuition, or spirit, as a guide.

If you feel drawn to perform simple ceremonies and rituals yourself when you are adding to or taking an item from your medicine bag, then do as the Algonquian did and follow your intuition. Remember that if you work from a perspective of love and respect—both for yourself and for all creation—whatever words or actions you use to invoke your ceremony cannot be incorrect. Such ceremonies come from the heart and are unique to each individual. Simply show your respect, honor creation—and creation will in turn respect and honor you.

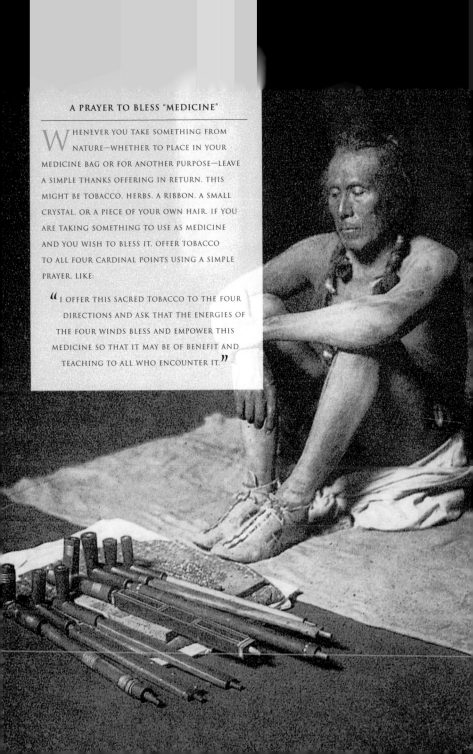

A PRAYER TO BLESS "MEDICINE"

Whenever you take something from nature—whether to place in your medicine bag or for another purpose—leave a simple thanks offering in return. This might be tobacco, herbs, a ribbon, a small crystal, or a piece of your own hair. If you are taking something to use as medicine and you wish to bless it, offer tobacco to all four cardinal points using a simple prayer, like:

" I offer this sacred tobacco to the four directions and ask that the energies of the four winds bless and empower this medicine so that it may be of benefit and teaching to all who encounter it. **"**

WE OWN NOTHING

One of the reasons why there was conflict over land rights between the white settlers and the Algonquian was because the Algonquian did not understand the concept of owning land in the same way that Europeans did. The Algonquian understood that in reality we own nothing. To them, it seemed preposterous that someone could be so naïve as to assume that he or she could take anything from this world without giving something of themselves in exchange. They knew that the Creator was the real owner of everything, who could instruct the thunder beings to come down and destroy anything—or anyone—who acted in a way that was detrimental to others; and that if the white settlers tried to keep hold of their land, they would one day lose it—and history has shown that to be true.

The Native view that no one may keep what is not theirs, and that everything belongs to the Creator, deeply marked the character of the new Americans.

Everything you think you own is really only on loan to you, and learning nonattachment to physical things is fundamental to the Algonquian tradition and a prerequisite of all the higher schools of spiritual learning. The items that the Algonquian kept in their medicine bags were not long-term possessions but were continually changing, as the Algonquian drew strength from these artifacts and then passed them on to someone else. The more you try to hold on to physical things (including other humans), the more enslaved you will become to them and the more your power will be lost. The Algonquian knew this and spoke of it in their legends.

THE POWER OF GIVING

The love with which you give a gift to another person is also a form of "medicine": it teaches the power of giving for the sheer pleasure of it. This in turn teaches us not to be selfish. Selfishness and greed are two of the major root causes of illness in the western world and, as the Algonquian well knew, ill health begins with unhealthy thinking.

All illness and "dis-ease"—whether physical, emotional, or spiritual—was regarded as a sign that your body was trying to teach you something. To put it another way, illness is your body's way of telling you that you are doing something wrong. Once you have learned what that is, and corrected it, you no longer need to manifest the illness.

The act of giving is itself a gift that we can give to ourselves. Giving can become an art and leads to a healthy mind and happiness for oneself and others.

Our modern lives are so cluttered with distractions that we often fail to notice such things and ignore the medicine that is right in front of our eyes. Perhaps if we simplified our lives, we would once more begin to find the significance of the lessons that are presented to us. By opening ourselves in this way, we might become wiser and healthier individuals. This is real medicine.

ALGON AND THE STAR MAIDEN

Algon was a Chippewa, one of the Algonquian peoples, and a keen and skilled hunter. One day he was out walking when he came upon a strange circle cut into the grass. It looked as if the grass had been trampled flat by thousands of tiny feet, and yet there were no footprints to be seen. Now, Algon had never seen a fairy ring before and, intrigued, he decided to hide in the long grass for a while to see if he could discover how it had been formed. Within a few minutes he heard strange music. It seemed to come from above his head and, looking up, Algon saw a basket made of osier reed descending from the sky. In the basket were seated twelve beautiful maidens, and the music that he heard was their voices as they sang their magical songs.

When the basket neared the ground, the maidens jumped out and began to dance around the ring with an elegance and beauty the like of which Algon had never seen. One particular maiden, the smallest of the group, transfixed Algon and he vowed in his mind to own her. She was a slight, vivacious creature so delicate-looking that Algon thought one breath would blow her away.

Algon suddenly felt a wild passion rising up within him, and in an instant he made a grab for the dainty girl. But the pretty creatures were too quick for him, and she eluded his grasp. Before he could gather himself for another try, all twelve maidens had returned to their basket and were now well out of his reach. He watched in anguish as the basket ascended to the tune of the maidens' unearthly songs, carrying his Star Maiden with it.

The following day, Algon could not get the Star Maiden out of his mind and vowed even more firmly to himself that he must have her. He returned to the fairy ring long before the hour of the maidens' arrival and once again secreted himself in the long grass.

Patiently he waited, and by and by he heard the first faint tones of a fairy song. Down came the twelve maidens in their basket, and round and round the ring they danced with furious speed. Again Algon made a desperate lunge for the girl of his choice—and again she eluded him.

"Let us stay," said one of the Star Maidens. "Perhaps this human wishes to teach us one of his earthly dances." But the youngest sister felt Algon's desire to own her and entreated the others to leave.

Algon returned home more unhappy than ever. At first light, he returned once more to the ring. Looking around for some way of disguising himself, he came upon a hollow log and found within it a family of mice sleeping soundly. With great deftness and gentleness, he carried the log to the ring and placed it there. Then, using all the magic charms from his medicine bag, he turned himself into a mouse and hid with the other mice inside the log.

Later that day, when the osier basket descended, the maidens danced their dance as merrily as ever, until the youngest sister spied the log (which had not been there the day before) and turned to flee. Her sisters laughed at her fear and tried to reassure her by turning the log over. At this, the mice awoke and scampered out in fright. Algon ran too, for he had fallen asleep waiting for the maidens. Now the Star Maidens had a liking for mouse skins and pursued the mice, killing all of them except Algon. As the youngest sister was about to kill him, Algon returned himself to his normal shape and captured the maiden. Her sisters flew in terror, leaving Algon to carry his prize back to his village.

When Algon arrived home with the Star Maiden, he married her and by his kindness and gentleness soon won her affection and she bore him a son. Algon loved his son and his wife and was totally devoted to them. However, the Star Maiden secretly cried at the loss of her freedom, yearning for her home.

One day, while she was out with her son, the Star Maiden made a basket out of osiers. Gathering some flowers for the Star People, she took her child and began to sing the magic songs that she recalled. Slowly the basket rose from the earth and she returned to her own country, where she was welcomed by the king, her father.

Algon's grief was great when he found that his wife and child had left him, but he had no means of following them. Every day he would go to the ring and wait for his wife to return, but, as the years passed, there was no sign of her, and Algon was left alone, a sad and pitiful man.

AFTERWORD

There seems to be no clearly defined place for this book to end; it is the story of a people called the Algonquian, but they were such a diverse community that we have only touched upon an account of their time and dealt with only a small fraction of the many nations. There is so much more that could be told—the stories, histories, and accounts of these tribes, if fully recorded, could go on indefinitely.

The past of the Algonquian is still coming to light as this book is being written; the influence that they have on today's world is still strong. We have seen in *The Friendship Pack* evidence of the significant role that they played in the formation of the twentieth-century world, as well as the ways in which their concept of life—of coexistence with their fellow humans and the importance of nature—can be of continuing value to us in our daily lives.

Words from the Algonquian language can be found in the names of places in which we live or might visit—places such as Massachusetts (named after the Massachuset people who once lived there), Manhattan (the island that is part of New York City), and Connecticut (from the Algonquian word *quinnectikut*, meaning a long tidal river).

However, the influence of the Algonquian people does not end there—it extends into many more significant areas of our lives.

Chief Powhatan's mantle: this deerskin decorated with shell patterns was owned by Chief Powhatan in Virginia. Who next may take up the mantles of the Native chiefs?

WORDS WITH ALGONQUIAN ORIGINS

THE FOLLOWING WORDS THAT ARE IN COMMON USE HAVE THEIR ROOTS IN THE ALGONQUIAN LANGUAGE:

TOBOGGAN A LONG, NARROW SLED THAT IS USED FOR SLIDING OVER ICE AND SNOW.

SQUASH A VEGETABLE OF THE GOURD VARIETY AND ONE OF THE ALGONQUIAN "THREE SISTERS;" EXAMPLES INCLUDE ACORN SQUASH, BUTTERNUT SQUASH, AND PUMPKIN.

POWWOW A GATHERING OF PEOPLE TO DANCE, CELEBRATE, OR GENERALLY SOCIALIZE.

SIOUX LITERALLY "A LITTLE VIPER, TO BE KILLED QUICKLY." A CURSE OR DEFAMATORY NAME BY WHICH THE LAKOTA, DAKOTA, AND NAKOTA CAME TO BE KNOWN.

TOTEM AN ITEM FROM THE NATURAL WORLD—OFTEN AN ANIMAL THAT IS OBSERVED AS A TEACHER OF THE WAY TO LIVE. ANIMAL TOTEMS (OR PARTS OF THEM) ARE FREQUENTLY FOUND ON MEDICINE ITEMS AND IN MEDICINE BAGS.

WIGWAM A TYPE OF PERMANENT HOME OR DWELLING COMMON TO THE EASTERN ALGONQUIAN.

ESKIMO LITERALLY "EATER OF RAW FISH." A TERM FOR THE PEOPLES LIVING NEAR THE ARCTIC CIRCLE IN CANADA, GREENLAND, AND RUSSIA.

MOCCASIN A TYPE OF SOFT LEATHER SHOE TRADITIONALLY WORN BY THE ALGONQUIAN.

MUGWUMP SOMEONE WHO REMAINS ALOOF OR DISTANCES THEMSELVES FROM PARTY POLITICS.

PAPOOSE A SMALL CHILD OR BABY.

TOMAHAWK A LIGHT HAND AX.

SQUAW A WOMAN. LITERAL MEANING FEMALE PUDENDA; A TERM HURLED AT EUROPEAN WOMEN WHO HAD SPREAD VENEREAL DISEASES TO THE ALGONQUIAN PEOPLES.

CAUCUS A GROUP OF PEOPLE WITH A COMMON INTEREST; NOW OFTEN USED FOR A LOCAL COMMITTEE OR FACTION OF A POLITICAL PARTY OR ORGANIZATION.

The openness of the Algonquian culture and the friendships that they offered to the first European settlers in the New World have become traits to which many peoples in modern times have aspired. The lessons they have taught us are still being offered today by many of their descendants.

There is a story from the Delaware tribe that has been retold for many years. The Delaware were once considered by many other Algonquian to be the grandfather nation, and their story (*see opposite*) seems to form an appropriate endnote for this book.

The story that is this book is not a new one, but rather the retelling of a story that has been related for many years in the history books and children's stories of today's civilized world. Sometimes the retelling of old stories in a different way helps people. Perhaps our retelling of this ancient story will help you.

Could we learn to manage our world better by approaching it in the manner that the Native Americans did? Perhaps their medicine will teach us the medicine we have yet to learn.

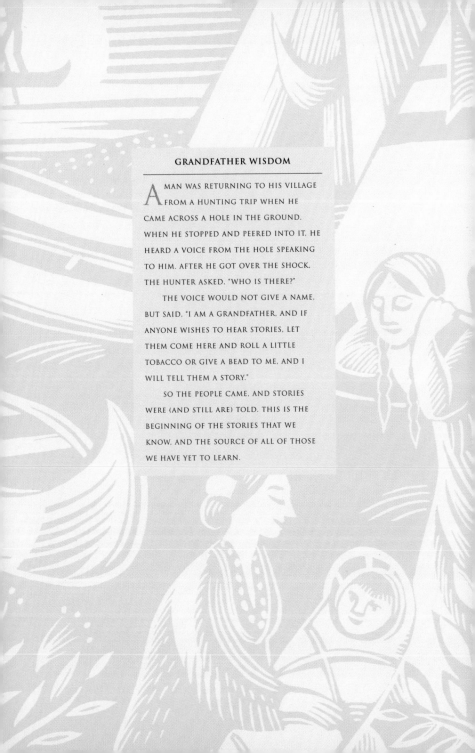

GRANDFATHER WISDOM

A MAN WAS RETURNING TO HIS VILLAGE FROM A HUNTING TRIP WHEN HE CAME ACROSS A HOLE IN THE GROUND. WHEN HE STOPPED AND PEERED INTO IT, HE HEARD A VOICE FROM THE HOLE SPEAKING TO HIM. AFTER HE GOT OVER THE SHOCK, THE HUNTER ASKED, "WHO IS THERE?"

THE VOICE WOULD NOT GIVE A NAME, BUT SAID, "I AM A GRANDFATHER, AND IF ANYONE WISHES TO HEAR STORIES, LET THEM COME HERE AND ROLL A LITTLE TOBACCO OR GIVE A BEAD TO ME, AND I WILL TELL THEM A STORY."

SO THE PEOPLE CAME, AND STORIES WERE (AND STILL ARE) TOLD. THIS IS THE BEGINNING OF THE STORIES THAT WE KNOW, AND THE SOURCE OF ALL OF THOSE WE HAVE YET TO LEARN.

1000 – 1529

c. 1000 Leif Ericsson, a Norse explorer, sails west from Greenland and lands with thirty-five companions in North America, calling it Vinland when he discovers grape vines growing there

1492 Christopher Columbus sails and makes the second European contact with Native Americans

Columbus made four great voyages in the small carracks or seafaring ships of his day.

1497 John Cabot makes the first English landing in the "New World;" no contact with Natives is made

1498 Vasco da Gama makes landfall at Calcutta, proving that there is a way to reach Asia, by sea, from Europe

1530 – 1589

1534 Jacques Cartier discovers the St. Lawrence River and is warmly welcomed by a group of Micmac—possibly the first direct contact by an Algonquian people with Europeans

1558 Elizabeth I is crowned Queen of England

Elizabeth was one of the great patrons of voyages of discovery

1583 Humphrey Gilbert receives the first English charter for a colony in the New World; it is established in Newfoundland, but is abandoned the same year

1590 – 1619

1590 White returns to Roanoke with supplies, but finds the colony abandoned, with no trace of the colonists

1602 Bartholomew Gosnold sails to northern "Virginia"; he finds an abundance of cod in a bay there and names the adjoining land Cape Cod

1603 James VI of Scotland succeeds to the English throne and becomes James I of England

1606 The Virginia Company is formed under James I and is then divided into the London Virginia Co. and the Plymouth Virginia Co.; these companies then subdivide the eastern seaboard into North Virginia (Delaware to Maine) under the Plymouth Co. and South Virginia (Delaware to Georgia) under the London Co.

The Portuguese da Gama traveled under the patronage of Manoel I.

1504 The French begin to fish the coastal waters off Newfoundland

1509 Henry VIII is crowned King of England

1524 Giovanni da Verrazano, sailing on behalf of France in search of a northwest passage to Asia, maps the east coast of North America from Carolina to Newfoundland

1584 Walter Raleigh is issued a royal patent by Queen Elizabeth I to explore foreign lands; Arthur Barlowe and Philip Amadus, sailing on behalf of Raleigh, report on the first meeting with the Powhatan

1585 Raleigh names all the land from the Carolinas to Newfoundland "Virginia," after England's "virgin" queen, Elizabeth I; for this, he receives a knighthood

1585 The first Roanoke colony is founded

1586 Roanoke fails and is abandoned

1587 The second Roanoke colony is established by John White, who then returns to England for supplies; Mary White (his granddaughter) is the first English child to be born in North America

1607 Jamestown, the first successful English colony, is established; late in the year John Smith is saved by Pocahontas, and invaluable friendships are established with the Powhatan

1609 Henry Hudson, an English captain sailing for the Dutch, finds what is now New York harbor

1610 Hudson, sailing now for England, finds the bay that is to be known thereafter as Hudson Bay

1612 John Rolfe develops tobacco as a cash crop at Jamestown

1614 Pocahontas, with her father's blessing, marries Rolfe

Pocahontas, seen here in distinctly European guise.

1620-1779

1620 The Plymouth Co. sends to what was then known as North Virginia a group of separatists fleeing religious persecution

1621 Samoset, a local Algonquian chief, warmly welcomes the "Pilgrims" and introduces them to other Native Americans who befriend them

1626 Peter Minuit is given permission to maintain New Amsterdam as a permanent colonial town on Manhattan Island

1664 The English take New Netherlands from the Dutch and rename New Amsterdam, New York

1681 William Penn, in the first treaty with the Delaware people, establishes Pennsylvania

1689 The outbreak of the "French and Indian War," in which the British use the Iroquois and the French use the Huron (Algonquian) to fight over control of North America

1780-1889

1783 The last of the British troops surrender and England officially recognizes the United States' independence; a period of multiple relocations begins for the Delaware Nation

The Declaration of Independence was signed by representatives of all the states.

1804-5 Meriwether Lewis and William Clark explore the upper regions of the Louisiana Purchase and find friendly allies among the Algonquian farthest west (the Cheyenne and Blackfoot)

1837 Queen Victoria starts her long period as ruler of Great Britain

1890-2000

1890 The United States declares that within its own territories there is no longer any "frontier"

1912 The British Liner *Titanic*, which is supposed to be unsinkable, strikes an iceberg and is lost off Newfoundland

The Titanic: *in its time, the world's greatest disaster at sea.*

1929 Wall Street's stock exchange crashes, causing millions of shares to becomes worthless in a matter of hours

1736 Conrad Weiser extends Pennsylvania through his friendship with the Iroquois

1756–63 The Seven Years War takes place in Europe

1760 Beginning of the reign of George III as King of Great Britain and Ireland

1775 Daniel Boone founds Boonesborough in Kentucky, beginning British colonial expansion westward across the Appalachian Mountains

1776 English colonies declare independence from Crown rule—the United States is born

1778 The Delaware, continuing their tradition of friendship, become the first Native Nation to make a treaty with the new United States; Continental Congress, the U.S. government, proposes the formation of a fourteenth state that will be populated only by Native Americans and will be led by the Delaware Nation

1848 Gold is discovered in California, precipitating a rush westward of 80,000 would-be prospectors, with even more arriving from all over the globe

1861–5 United States Civil War: General Stand Waite, a Cherokee, leads the Indian Regiment in which there are Algonquian troops; they fight for the Confederate States (the South)

The majority of the so-called "49-ers" were unsuccessful.

1866 End of the official relocation period of the Delaware Nation, although some tribes will continue to relocate until the turn of the next century; the Delaware are now given a place in the Indian Territory (Oklahoma)

1959 Hawaii is proclaimed the fiftieth state

1967 Algonquian are among the Native Americans who occupy Alcatraz Island, trying to turn it into a cultural Native center

Since the mid-1960s, the fight for political recognition of Native American rights has gathered force.

1979 The Bureau of Indian Affairs "administratively terminates" the Delaware Nation

1996 The termination of the Delaware is reversed and they regain "official" recognition of their existence